What Leaders Are Saying About
The H.U.M.A.N. Approach

This book! Kristen Moreland's A More H.U.M.A.N Approach to Educational Leadership is more than a necessary read for educational leaders; it is transformational. Grounded in research and embedded with nuggets of wisdom, applicable insight and opportunities for reflection, Dr. Moreland has written a gem that empowers educational leaders to remember not only why we teach and lead, but who. As such, she reminds us that with a H.U.M.A.N. approach we can cultivate connection, seek solutions and create conditions for success that optimize the learning environment and honor the human beings with whom we interact daily. This author's compassion, knowledge and organizational style contributes to the page-turner that is this book. A More H.U.M.A.N Approach to Educational Leadership was designed to "help school and district leaders bring humanity back to education" and it does exactly that- with relevance, practical strategies and tangible hope!

Michelle L. Trujillo, M.Ed
Author, Speaker, Consultant

Kristen Moreland's groundbreaking new book, A More H.U.M.A.N. Approach to School Leadership will bring new hope, new opportunities, and new vistas into "this place called school." Examples, illustrations, vignettes, and witty epigrams from luminaries across the globe and throughout time demonstrate just "how" it can be done. Cleverly written and in a manner most apropos for leaders at ALL levels, Dr. Moreland hones in on what school leaders worry about the most— "time and space." And so, as one dives into these pages of what it means to be a great leader, they begin to see the kaleidoscopic array of "how to" with a much more human-centered approach. In short, Kristen Moreland has crystallized for neophyte and veteran leaders alike, a panoply of leadership qualities and approaches that sit in easy reach.

Dr. Franklyn Bass
Former Superintendent/Adjunct Professor of Educational Leadership

A practical companion on your educational leadership journey. Not only is A More H.U.M.A.N Approach to Educational Leadership H.U.M.A.N. filled with novel advice and things to try for leaders in the education system, it is built on an elegant system of profound principles. This book is a unique approach to a crucial modern challenge: creating more human experiences for everyone in the school system - educators, administrators and students alike. I hope the ideas in this book find fertile soil to grow in schools around the world.

Naryan Wong
Author, Leadership Consultant, Systems Steward

In A More H.U.M.A.N. Approach to Educational Leadership, Kristen Moreland masterfully invites educational leaders to rethink their approach to daily challenges. This essential read is centered on the foundational principles of leading with self-awareness, kindness, vision, accountability, and trust. Moreland skillfully intertwines theory with practical application through a series of engaging activities, lessons, and reflections designed to inspire profound transformation within organizations.
Her compelling insights empower leaders to cultivate more joyful and inclusive communities where collaboration flourishes, and innovation thrives. In an era where authentic leadership is paramount, this book is a beacon of hope and guidance. It truly deserves a place on every leader's bookshelf, as it not only enhances professional practices but ultimately serves the greater good of humanity. Embrace the H.U.M.A.N. way and unlock the potential within yourself and your organization – this is a reading experience you won't want to miss.

Dr. Lois Costa
Superintendent/Adjunct Professor of Educational Leadership

A More H.U.M.A.N Approach to Educational Leadership by Dr. Kristen Moreland is an essential guide for educators and leaders who strive to transform learning environments by first reflecting on their own practices and approaches. This well-organized, easy to read book offers practical strategies and applications as well as suggestions for implementation. A bonus is the storytelling elements that are woven together with research and experiences from practitioners around the globe. The various scenarios that are provided and additional resources are invaluable, as are the reflection opportunities. This is a must-read for all who want to approach their work in a spirit of openness and humanity.

Jan Yost
Former Principal, Consultant & Author

A More
H.U.M.A.N.
Approach to Educational Leadership

Kristen Moreland, Ed.D.

Foreword by Jennifer Abrams

A More H.U.M.A.N. Approach to Educational Leadership
By Kristen Moreland, Ed.D.

Published by EDLINKS® Press
PO Box 205
Essex Junction, VT 05453
United States of America
edlinkspress@edlinks.com

ISBN: 979-8-9897654-8-5

First Printing, 2024

H   Hone Compassion

U   Understand One's
Identity As A Leader

M   Make Meaning For Others
While Motivated By A Vision

A   Anticipate And Acknowledge
The Unknown

N   Nurture Trust To Create A
Sense of Belonging

Contents

Foreword

Abraham Joshua Heschel, a leading Jewish theologian and philosopher, once said, "We don't need more textbooks. We need more text people." Kristen Moreland has written a book for those of us who want to be that 'text person.' That human. Through her book, she speaks to the many ways we can bring even more of our humanity into our work in schools.

I know from working with her that she is the perfect person to be writing a book such as *A More H.U.M.A.N. Approach to Educational Leadership*. She is a text person who brings light and humanity to every interaction, and through your reading of this book you too will find ways to bring out more of your humane text person-ness as well. I met Kristen in a workshop I was facilitating for international educators entitled 'The Heart of Teaching: Beyond Content.' The week's work was all about asking ourselves, "Who is the "I" that is teaching?" And "Am I living out loud the "I" who I want to be as an educator?" Kristen was a smiling face throughout the week, engaged with her colleagues, thoughtful in her contributions, and awake to the essentialness of the conversation. She knew decades ago that her work was about teaching students subject matter, of course, but it was even more so to model for them how to be a humane human being.

Decades later, after bringing her light and humanity to students and schools on several continents Kristen has brought her text personness into the world yet again. And funnily enough, now in a text form! With this book, readers will find support, solace, and encouragement to grow their leadership capacity to become that humane human being in whatever leadership role they are in. Kristen is an authentic and approachable author, who guides us through the windy roads of educational leadership yet always keeping us grounded in our values of being human. Being compassionate. Being inclusive. Being a text person.

What I appreciate about this book is that I found the text so honest and real. By letting us connect to the concepts through a coaching conversation, a relatable and vulnerable interaction, we see the humanity that Kristen brings to the elements that you will learn in the acronym H.U.M.A.N. She encourages her readers to see themselves as fallible. Like her coachee, we, the readers, are also sometimes "in fallback," not able to always be our best, most mature selves. And it's normal! It's okay! With her writing, she gives us real world challenges we might (and often do) face and provides us with support— protocols and practices to assist us as we strive and develop. Kristen is a coach in her 'being' and in her writing. (And as a former English teacher, I also love the quotations she intersperses throughout too!)

Kristen and I share the belief that schools need to not only support child development but also adult development. Kristen, in her many years of working in schools worldwide and with many educators understands the essentialness of this work in adult development at a global level. Our growth and development aren't just 'a nice thing to focus on when or if we have time.' It is critical that we develop our leadership capacities in the most urgent of ways. This book is a support to us as we go on our journey of developing into an even better educational leader. Kristen is right there with us, a text person who is providing us a H.U.M.A.N. approach with which to see how and where we can grow.

I saw on Instagram a quote from @mrscowmansclassroom—"Someone is learning how to be a person by watching you. Let that sink in." I have watched Kristen Moreland for decades now. She is the real deal. H.U.M.A.N. in her bones. As you are reading the book, you too will feel her humanity. Kristen writes, "[T]his book summarizes the work I have been doing, and the work that I hope somehow is making a difference." It has made a difference to me, and it will to you. Enjoy.

Jennifer Abrams
Educational Consultant and Author

Acknowledgments

During an interview in 2013, Archbishop Desmond Tutu explained the term "Ubuntu" to mean "the essence of humanity." He elaborates on the definition further, stating, "My humanity is bound up in yours. I am, only because you are." A more H.U.M.A.N. approach embodies this philosophy, and it exists because of the support, encouragement, and love of so many incredible people.

To my global network of support: whether you were a reader of an early draft, a part of my dissertation process, or a consistent positive and encouraging voice, your ferocious belief in me and this topic re-energized me during each conversation. I am so grateful for each and everyone of you. Your perspectives and ways of being are aspirational models for my own scholarship and leadership. Truly, *"I am, only because you are."*

To the entire team at EDLINKS® and EDLINKS® Press, thank you for helping me overcome my imposter syndrome to help make this book a reality! Your encouragement and insights have truly changed the way I see and make sense of the world. I am so thankful for our collaboration! Additionally, to all of the authors who gave their permission to share their work in pursuit of spreading the H.U.M.A.N. approach, your collaboration is such a gift!

Behind the scenes has always been Jeff and Joy. Joy, the best four-legged writing companion ever, made sure we always took breaks to be on the trail. And Jeff, who made sure everything was taken care of so I could focus on the writing and creating, and who never dismissed an anxiety-ridden moment or an urgent return to the computer to "just check one thing." You removed obstacles and barriers, and kept me "fed and watered." Your unconditional love, humor, fresh bread, and company on the trail are things I cherish more than you will ever know.

Most importantly, none of this would exist without the leaders in education who take a H.U.M.A.N. approach. The wisdom of educators from around the globe is evident in these pages. Thank you for your time, wisdom, and all the gifts you share with those in your spheres of influence. The difference you make is unquantifiable, and it is an honor to witness how you are bringing humanity back to education.

Introduction

School shootings. Divisive concepts laws. Accusations of "indoctrination." Curriculum and book bannings. Violence and aggression at school board meetings. TikTok attacks on school staffs. The number of negative news stories and social media posts regarding the state of education today is exhausting and overwhelming.

And yet. Even with the risks of negative impacts on their physical and emotional well-being, educators around the world continue to show up and do their best for their students.

Every single day.

When I think about who I am as an educator, leader, and human being, this quotation from the 13th-century poet Rumi has been a guide and touchstone for the work I do: *Be a lamp, or a lifeboat, or a ladder. Help someone's soul heal. Walk out of your house like a shepherd.* Though

"Be a lamp, or a lifeboat, or a ladder. Help someone's soul heal. Walk out of your house like a shepherd."

~Rumi

talking about someone's 'soul' in terms of instructional practice may seem incongruent, for me, they are intertwined. While serving a large urban district as an instructional coach, I knew that technically, my job was supposed to be about helping teachers improve their instructional practices. I was trained in all the techniques—from helping teachers know where to stand for prime effectiveness,[1] how to get kids' attention, how to differentiate assignments, and how to look at exit tickets to make changes to the next day's lessons. But if a teacher was processing the fight that just happened in class or an urgent email from a concerned parent, I needed to support the teacher as a human being first.[2]

The great educator and author Parker Palmer, wrote, "We teach who we are."[3] When we are emotionally regulated and can see the good in the world around us, that impacts how we show up in the classroom. So does the opposite. Our role as educators is to teach and model these basic skills for our students to help them grow into the adults our collective future needs and deserves. School and district leaders also need to be intentional in modeling these basic skills to help shape a culture that is committed to the development of good human beings at all ages.

Throughout my experiences in schools on four different continents, one thing has become abundantly clear: the adult culture of a school matters more than we realize. Today, there are countless books, blogs, and workshops dedicated to reversing what has become, generally speaking, a very demoralizing time to be an educator. My friend Jennifer Abrams writes, "As educators in a human-centered field, we live out loud our elemental beliefs in the worth and dignity of all human beings."[4] Let this serve as a reminder and call to action to elevate our collective humanity.

In his book, *Cultures of Thinking in Action: 10 Mindsets to Change our Teaching and our Students' Learning*, Ron Ritchhart offers educators these questions when considering their purpose: "1) Who are our students becoming as thinkers and learners as a result of their time with us, and 2) What do we want the students we teach to be like as adults?"[5] The answer to these questions is often found in what Ritchhart calls "institutional mirroring," or the idea that the way teachers are treated will directly impact how these same teachers treat their students. Teacher behavior, or the adult culture of a school, is directly linked to the actions and beliefs of building and district-level leadership.

I have sat with far too many educators who needed space to cry because of how they were being treated at school–*by the other adults* (and I include myself as one of the criers in this count). Seeing this fragile state of the teachers' emotional well-being, in 2017 I created the Instagram account, *Educatorsforhumanity*. My vision: to bring humanity back to education. I wanted people to reconnect with the joy and passion that brought them into this career in the first place; especially for educators who may have lost sight of those ideals along the way. A lofty goal, for sure, but I thought if I could offer a little bit of light on those dark days; if I could let teachers know: *I see you. You are valued. You are doing a good job,* maybe that would help heal our fractured humanity just a little bit. It doesn't seem like a lot, I know, but I hoped it was a little like the *Starfish* story.

Do you remember this one?

"One day a man was walking along the beach when he noticed a boy picking up and gently throwing things into the ocean. Approaching the boy, he asked, 'Young man, what are you doing?'
'Throwing starfish back into the ocean. The surf is up and the tide is going out. If I don't throw them back, they'll die,' the boy replied.
'Do you realize there are miles of miles of beach and hundreds and hundreds of starfish? You can't make any difference.'
After listening politely, the boy bent down to pick up another starfish and threw it into the surf. Then, he smiled at the man and said, 'I made a difference to that one.'"

~Loren Eiseley

As my role as an instructional coach began to include working with more principals and other building administrators, I gained greater insight into the impact a school leader could have in how the adults engage not just with their students in the classroom, but with each other. Schools can be highly stressful places though, and as is the case with anyone, the more stress we experience impacts how we show up in the world. The work of running a school is multilayered and complex. When leaders are so overwhelmed they aren't sleeping and subsisting on leftover donuts from the staff room, it becomes significantly more difficult to show up as your best self. So, I began supporting leaders through the lens of their reactions to stress, resilience process, and emotional regulation. To use a sports coach analogy, I would often tell those I worked with our time together was like a "time-out" or a "water break" (sometimes, quite literally); that it was an opportunity to pause, to take a look at what's going on, and make a plan to get back into the game, refreshed and fortified. These moments were all supporting my vision of bringing humanity back to education.

How the Approach Came to Life

School culture experts Steve Gruenert and Todd Whitaker[6] remind us that culture shifts can take years to implement. This is because culture is determined by values and beliefs. Our values and beliefs are formed over lifetimes of experiences. To change anything that is deeply embedded requires leaders to be fully committed to their efforts to bring about transformation. How can they do that? With so much research available on different types of positive leadership styles, I wondered which approach might best support a change in the adult culture of our schools. Transformational Leaders create the conditions for positive change and evolution, and Authentic Leaders bring their whole selves to the table and invite you to do the same. There are the Servant Leaders, who truly live to empower others, and my absolute favorite, the Heliotropic Leaders: the ones who serve as a light shining and life-giving force for others. In the multi-faceted world of education, is it possible to embrace elements of them all?

The more I researched, the more I noticed how similar and overlapping many of the ideas of the various leadership theories are as they apply to different contexts. The themes of inclusivity, connection, and personal growth began to show up again and again. The four domains of emotional intelligence (self-awareness, self-management, social awareness, and relationship management)[7] also seem to align with the core elements of many leadership theories. As I began to categorize all of these different ideas, a new picture began emerging on its own: suggestions on how we might actually blend all of these ideas together to truly honor our shared humanity.

"We teach who we are."

-Parker Palmer

A *Harvard Business School Review* article notes that truly human-centered leadership is more than just soft skills. It "requires having a genuine intention to help each person succeed and find fulfillment at work, along with a disciplined approach to effectively choosing and exhibiting the leadership behaviors appropriate for the individual and the context."[8] There are many other examples of human-centered leadership around the globe in the fields of business and education.[9,10] All of these organizations and individuals—as well as many others, including new ones popping up as you read this—are working to engage positive transformations in their organizations by making fundamental mindset shifts to emphasize one's levels of emotional intelligence and the power of human connection. These shifts have the potential to create a lasting ripple effect throughout multiple sectors of our global society. One can readily argue that these are unequivocally necessary forces in today's world of heightened anger and bitter divisiveness.

The H.U.M.A.N. approach to educational leadership weaves together a strengths-based perspective with insights from emotional intelligence and authentic, transformational, and heliotropic leadership philosophies. It draws from a variety of self-assessments and leadership competency rubrics from key thought leaders and institutions in the field of leadership.[11] Ultimately, It describes leaders who: ***Hone their Compassion, Understand their Identities as Leaders, Make Meaning for Others while Motivated by a Vision, Anticipate and Acknowledge the Unknown, and Nurture Trust to Create a Sense of Belonging.*** Here's a quick overview of what each element of the H.U.M.A.N. approach means to me:

H: *The H.U.M.A.N. approach asks leaders to '**hone their compassion.**'* Brené Brown says empathy is a tool of compassion,[12] and this is something we need to practice daily. According to the research, the major difference between empathy and compassion is action.[13] And when we hone something, we refine or sharpen it. So, to hone our compassion, we need to take action that will help us gain a deeper understanding of everyone around us, especially those we might not agree with. These regular refinements can lead to deeper connections and stronger relationships with the adults on our teams and in our buildings, and ultimately, a more positive culture.

U: *Using the H.U.M.A.N. approach, leaders don't just strive to understand others but take intentional steps to **understand their identities as leaders** in their schools or districts.* With a deeper understanding of who we are and how we make sense of our world, we can separate ourselves from drama and chaos long enough to consider where our reactions are coming from. Though this reflective process is not always easy, knowing who we are can help us learn from decisions we have made in the past to inform those we'll make in the future. We can use those insights to make changes that help us grow, modeling this practice for those around us.

M: *In the H.U.M.A.N. approach, leaders **make meaning for others while they are motivated by a personal vision.*** Trust guru Steven Covey reminds us we need to "connect WITH people and TO purpose."[14] No matter what motivates us to do the work we do, we are all driven by something deeper that inspires us to show up each day and do what we can to make the world a better place. By keeping an eye on the greater vision you are hoping to achieve, you can help others make sense of what often seems chaotic and convoluted. This brings to life another element of the H.U.M.A.N. approach.

A: ***Anticipate and acknowledge the unknown.*** In the H.U.M.A.N. approach, we know that not everything will go the way we plan, and we're ok with that. Education in general, and schools in particular, are complex, multilayered systems, and we have to both anticipate —or be ready for—and acknowledge or be ok with not knowing what the future holds. This is about our positionality towards change. Is it something you hide from? Or something you embrace?

N: *With a H.U.M.A.N. approach, leaders constantly **nurture trust to create a sense of belonging** for everyone in their spheres of influence.* Building and sustaining relationships in our schools and districts—student to student, student to adult, and adult to adult— needs to be our number one priority. We all know that trust is essential in this endeavor. When people dare to trust the connections they have with others, a feeling of belonging is enhanced. This feeling allows individuals to truly thrive.

Now. Is taking a H.U.M.A.N. approach to your leadership going to immediately solve all of your problems? Probably not. It is essential to note that all of the elements of the approach represent aspirational states. For most of us mere mortals, it's pretty close to impossible to live out loud all of these ideas, every day, in the face of all manner of attacks that seem to confront most educational leaders. Yet with a commitment to practicing this approach, leaders in education can model a way of being that just might inspire a better future for all of us. This is how we can strengthen humanity through education.

Synchronicity

Sometimes, there is a lesson people so desperately need, the Universe puts out multiple calls to action from a variety of places. While I was working on my research, Dr. Jennifer Nash was creating her own human framework for the world of business. She defines human leadership this way:

Human Leaders behave in ways that build, nurture, and sustain relational connection. They create cultures that are healthy, preserve people's integrity, and promote risk-taking. They give trust first to get trust. Human Leaders build relationships through effective communication, authentic connection, and caring. They bring positive relational energy, compassion, and shared vision to interactions with others. In essence, Human Leaders understand that connection and relationships drive engagement and commitment, which in turn delivers performance.[15]

She summarizes this definition with these key terms: **hearing, understanding, mattering, appreciating, iNspiring, and seeing (HUMANS)**. Each one of these ideas is embedded within the *H.U.M.A.N. Approach to Educational Leadership*. This serves as both a reminder and validation that no matter your chosen field, a united, humanity-supporting front is of utmost importance right now.

You can take the HLI™(Human Leader Index™) to assess your own areas of strength and opportunities for growth in the six core areas on Dr. Nash's website: https://drjennifernash.com/hli

Adult Development

Another thread in the fabric of the H.U.M.A.N. approach is the theory of adult development. A few years ago, I read an article about Robert Kegan's adult development theory, and it completely changed my interactions with the adults around me. It was like a light was finally turned on, and the behaviors of the people I worked with started to make so much sense. I began to read more by some of the key scholars in the field (Robert Kegan, Deborah Helsing, Lisa Lahey, Jennifer Garvey Berger, and Ellie Drago-Severson, just to name a few), and the implications of this theory for adults in schools felt like a call to action. Ultimately this theory comes down to adults continuing to grow and blossom into better versions of themselves while their capacity to see more complexity in the world is enhanced. To me, this seems like a worthwhile journey to take!

While I am still learning about this theory (and myself in relation to its wisdom!), here is a quick overview. The big idea is that adults can—and do—continue to develop long into their adult years. And, as adults grow and change, the way they make meaning in their lives also changes, allowing them to appreciate a fuller, more complex picture of the world around them as it comes into focus. This is often described using the language of "subject" and "object." In their book *Immunity to Change*, Robert Kegan and Lisa Lahey[16] describe this subject/object paradigm this way:

> *A way of knowing becomes more complex when it is able to look at what before it could only look through...if we want to increase mental complexity, we need to move aspects of our meaning-making from subject to object, to alter our mindset so*

that a way of knowing or making meaning becomes a kind of "tool" that we have (and can control or use) rather than something that has us (and therefore controls and uses us). (p. 51)

As school leaders face more challenging situations in their leadership, this perspective shift from subject to object will help them navigate many layers of complexity, leading to growth. Jennifer Garvey Berger writes, "Growing is when the form of our understanding changes; we often call this 'transformation.'"[17] Embracing the elements of the H.U.M.A.N. approach to leadership is a way to support this transformation, no matter where one is on their personal journey of development.

In Rober Kegan's adult development theory, our capacity as adults to make meaning of the world around us typically falls within four orders or stages. (There is an earlier developmental stage which typically applies to children and adolescents.) Research shows 13% of adults are in the self-sovereign mind,[17] or the second order. Those who live with a self-sovereign mind see only their own story (i.e. everything is all about them). Life in the self-sovereign world is very black and white. These individuals navigate the world without the benefit of other perspectives, or, sometimes, the understanding that there ARE other perspectives.

The third order in this theory is referred to as the *socialized mind*, or, to use Ellie Drago-Severson's term,[18] "the socialized way of knowing." Those who have grown into experiencing the world with a socialized mind have become integrated into their chosen society. They understand the rules and the customs and they have developed empathy and respect for those in their communities. These individuals are deeply connected to, and their success is often defined by, the ideas of those with whom they have aligned. Those with a socialized way of knowing fiercely cling to rules put forth by these authorities they deem important. According to the researchers I have mentioned, most adults live their lives with this socialized way of knowing, or in the third order.

But, there are those who move beyond that, and they continue to develop into the fourth order. This is called the *self-authoring mind* or way of knowing. This is a stage in which adults have the internal resources to create and use their beliefs as a guide. These adults think they are modeling what adults "should be."[17] They have the confidence to write their own story without looking for validation or guidance from others. While they can see other perspectives, adults with this way of knowing look to those other perspectives to validate their own. These adults are sure in their convictions, and they know where they are going. This confidence is a positive attribute, for sure. There are times though, when these folks are holding on to that self-authoring pen a little too tightly, and they aren't willing to take the constructive feedback necessary to really refine and enhance the stories they are writing about themselves.

And then, there is an even smaller percentage of adults who grow into the fifth order or the *self-transforming* mind. Robert Kegan[19] noted that his research has uncovered that most individuals don't reach this stage until they are at least 40. The self-transforming stage is a way of understanding the world in which people can hold multiple perspectives in their minds at once, remaining open to all possibilities. They can see and make sense of others' ways of knowing, causing them to lose their grip on their personal pen, so to speak. These are individuals who, Ellie Drago-Severson and her colleagues describe as having an "enhanced capacity for holding and being more—more inclusive, more connected, more than oneself alone."[20] This new level of awareness allows them to become, as adult development guru Jennifer Garvey Berger has noted, both the "writer and the written,"[21] taking in additional information to continue to grow and change their understanding of their experiences.

Let's let that sink in for a moment: *At this self-transforming stage, you become the writer AND the written.* Or, in the words of another one of my favorite quotes from Thich Nhat Hahn: *"Enlightenment is when the wave realizes it is the ocean."* This way of knowing is when we are reminded that there is something bigger than us out there, and that we are all just a tiny part of a vast universe of lived experiences and all of the shades of grey that exist.

A key point: The stages of adult development are a judgment free zone. Each order has its own strengths and opportunities for growth. Your journey is yours and yours alone. Only you can make sense of how you are experiencing the world in a way that your current context demands.

When We're Not On Top Of Our Game

But WAIT, there's a bit more. We can't talk about all of this growth without also recognizing that sometimes, real life gets in the way and that beautiful image of the wave and the ocean comes crashing to the shore. Sometimes, let's face it, there are moments when—and I'll only speak for myself here—I am not at my best. And that's ok. This is a state called fallback. According to author and researcher Valerie Livesay, "Fallback is the loss of options, of capacity, of ability to feel, behave, and think at the emotional and psychological level that we are normally (read: *optimally*) capable."[22] Livesay writes that sometimes in these moments we describe them by saying, *That wasn't me.* Because it's not—who you are right now. But it is someone you have been at some point in your journey. That's the thing about our development as adults. You don't "graduate" from each stage with a nice, neat separation. You grow and evolve, but you continue to take all of these pieces of you with you. And though the farther along you grow, you may see those other selves less and less, we have to recognize that they are still there. Sometimes, when we are triggered, someone other than the self we want to be showing the world might make an appearance.

While the H.U.M.A.N. approach offers positive and aspirational ways to manifest one's leadership capabilities, it does not ignore the actual humans that comprise a given team or collective staff. Schools and classrooms contain myriad personalities, moods, behaviors, and general ways of being influenced by individual experiences. In light of this, even the most well-intentioned leaders can—and do—experience periods of "fallback" when confronted with obstacles and challenges. Depending on the trigger and one's current way of making sense of the world, these periods of "fallback" could last the duration of a faculty meeting, or possibly even the course of an entire school year.

What if school leaders could be more self-aware in their personal moments of "fallback" and open to the lessons presented during these lapses? Or—even better—what if they had someone to process these reactions with? This is where working with a leadership coach can be a game changer. During their coaching sessions, leaders can build compassion for themselves as they take a deeper dive into how they are making sense of the world around them. This type of reflection and subsequent awareness are crucial to the work of leading today's schools.

Living the Approach Out Loud

While researching for this book, the readings and conversations I had served as both windows and mirrors to my personal experiences as an educational leader. I was able to peek into the lived experiences of others while simultaneously reflecting on my own ways of being in this role. The wisdom I gleaned echoed in my head while I went through challenging situations, and I now recognize I experience more moments of fallback than I previously realized—or was willing to admit! As I tried to live out loud the elements of the H.U.M.A.N. approach, I started to notice when others were struggling or soaring in these same areas. I believe that leaders can develop the skills within the H.U.M.A.N. approach IF they are made aware of them. But this is an ongoing process that requires daily maintenance, and someone to support you when "real life" gets in the way. A leadership coach can help. By engaging with a coach, school and district leaders can model their commitment to becoming the best version of themselves, and hopefully inspire the adult cultures of their organizations along the way.

At the time of this writing, there were over 600 million leadership resources available on the Internet. New articles, books, and research studies—not to mention other varieties of social media wisdom—seem to be added each second. More and more of these publications address how leaders can connect to those they work with via their own humanity. Clearly, there continues to be a need for this kind of content. Many of these resources offer practical suggestions for how to incorporate techniques that embrace a strengths-based mindset and positive presuppositions. Though none of these ideas are new, their volume is finally being magnified.

Bill Ayers wrote, "Teaching is at its heart an act of hope for a better future."[23] Yet this principle often gets lost in the endless complexity of each school day, to say nothing of larger political and social issues. By embodying the elements of the H.U.M.A.N. approach, educational leaders will be able to develop themselves and their organizations in service of what is most important: our collective humanity.

Why Should You Read This Book?

For the past decade or so, I have been kind of haunted by this question of how leaders in education are creating the conditions for their teachers to embrace the idea of being good people to each other. The 2023 Merrimack College Teacher survey asked participants an open-ended question regarding what school leaders needed to learn in the areas of teacher well-being. The results indicated that "aspiring administrators should learn to understand, support, care for, value, and listen to teachers."[24] This requires careful and attentive listening to fully understand each educator on our team and embrace the fullness of the new picture that begins to reveal itself. While budgeting issues or state mandates often take center stage, we cannot ignore the need for compassion and trust. These are key components of creating a culture of support and growth for everyone—adults included—in our schools. With more leaders in education embracing the H.U.M.A.N. approach, it is my hope that some of these negative trends plaguing our adult cultures will begin to dissipate.

So why should YOU read this book? This book is for leaders at all levels of education. Whether you are a building principal, a superintendent, a teacher leader, a district-level administrator, or any of the roles in between, this book is for you. Whether you have "positional authority" or "situational influence," this book is for you. Each chapter will take a deeper dive into the elements of the H.U.M.A.N. approach. You'll also have the opportunity to step inside a coaching session with a school leader who is trying to take a more H.U.M.A.N. approach with their leadership, but the reality of school life is throwing up some obstacles. This will give you a practical example of how the ideas embedded within each element of the H.U.M.A.N. approach show up in the daily lives of leaders in education.

Each coaching session's vignette is a compilation of my own personal experiences, either through direct participation or a blending of anecdotes from stories relayed by friends and colleagues from around the globe. Identifying details have been changed in order to protect the anonymity of individuals and schools. However, while I wish this were not the case, I have a feeling that you will connect with these stories as common examples of the collective school leadership experience.

Ultimately, though, I wrote this book for me. I need these reminders. As I continue to learn about adult development theory, I am keeping a metacognitive eye on how I am modeling the elements of the H.U.M.A.N. approach in my own leadership, as well as how they show up in the actions of others. I know I should be compassionate, and I am getting better at recognizing my triggers. I need daily reminders to pause and not react. But sometimes, there are those moments…and I have a feeling you experience them, too.

My essential takeaway is that this work is far from easy, and I experience fallback on a regular, sometimes daily, basis. However, this self-awareness has only strengthened my belief that the adult cultures in our schools matter significantly. Just as our teachers are committed to inspiring their students, educational leaders must also inspire their teachers, enhancing their well-being by encouraging them to turn toward the light to grow and develop into a bright future.

"Everybody needs a coach. Everyone. Coaching done well may be the most effective intervention designed for human performance."

~Atul Gawande

Some Thoughts On Coaching For School Leaders

I have also come to learn that not all school leaders have ever considered working with a leadership coach, let alone been given the opportunity. There is often the misconception that coaching is for when things are going wrong, or when someone needs to be "fixed." While this does happen far too often, the joy of coaching is found in the growth and development that comes from examining your own thinking to help you understand how you make sense of the world. The can lead to breakthrough moments that can be powerfully transformative (but even the small 'a-has' are pretty great). In their book, *Making Coaching Matter: Leading Continuous Improvement in Schools*, Sarah Woulfin and her colleagues claim that "coaching stands on the premise that each and every educator can—and should—learn, change, and improve."[25] The H.U.M.A.N. approach offers one framework in which to ground these coaching conversations to bring about real change in first ourselves, and then our schools.

We can't ignore the time obstacle for school leaders. Given the choice of fires that need to be put out at any given moment, how could there possibly be 45 minutes of uninterrupted time for self-reflection with someone who cares about helping you be your best self? Is that even a real job? I get it. The days are packed and you are probably triple booked most of the time. If not, that walkie-talkie is bound to announce a crisis any minute. But if you have found a few spare moments to read this at home, then, I hope you can make some connections with what is going on in your own leadership life, and maybe share your new insights with those on your team who might benefit from your wisdom.

Ultimately, this book was designed to help school and district leaders enhance our shared humanity, starting with themselves. And that, Dear Educator, is exactly why you need this book.

How To Use This Book

This book can be used in a variety of ways:

✔Use it by yourself as a place for reflection and insight.

✔Use it with your coach for even deeper exploration.

✔Use it with your team to create a ripple effect of the H.U.M.A.N. approach in our schools.

For your ease of application and readability, each chapter is designed the same way:

- A review of the descriptive statements for each element with some key terms to support your learning.

- An opportunity to consider what draws you to that particular element of the H.U.M.A.N. approach on a given day.

    Note: You can read this book in any order you want. Go cover to cover or pick a specific element that speaks to you and start there. Follow your heart. Listen to your gut. Pay attention to the signs around you. This is all about you.

- A brief snippet of a conversation between a school leader and her coach.

    Note: each conversation will start with "So, what's the most important thing for us to talk about today?" This is a question suggested by instructional coaching leader Jim Knight[26] as a way to empower the person being coached. I love this question, and I hope you see how effective it is!

- A short analysis of the coaching conversation to emphasize the connections to the H.U.M.A.N. approach.

- A review of the research that contributed to creating each element.

- A few reflection questions and space to write.

    Note: You will always see the question, "Considering all of this, who do you want to be, next?" This is another favorite of mine, a modification of a question posed by the aforementioned adult development expert, Jennifer Garvey Berger.[27]

THEN, Come The Opportunities.

At the end of each chapter, you will find some of my favorite protocols and practices I have collected and curated over the years. Undoubtedly, you have engaged in a few of these yourselves throughout your career in education. For each element of the approach, you will find:

- 5 Protocols and Practices for Developing Yourself

- 5 Protocols and Practices for Developing Your Team

    Some protocols and practices are good for both individuals and teams, and you'll see suggestions for how to adjust depending on your audience in these cases.

- 5 Resources to Keep Your Learning and Growing: Just a few of my favorites!

The "Opportunities" section contains a lot of different protocols. You have most likely encountered some of them. Here's an overview of what they are:

What is a Protocol? *From National School Reform Faculty*[28]:

"Protocols are structured processes and guidelines to promote meaningful, efficient communication, problem-solving, and learning. Protocols give time for active listening and reflection, and ensure that all voices in the group are heard and honored. Using protocols appropriately in meetings with colleagues, students, parents, and others helps you build the skills and the culture necessary for productive collaborative work." *https://www.nsrfharmony.org*

Finally, there are some "key takeaways" and more space for reflection. My hope is that you use this as a workbook or journal. I encourage you to underline, highlight, take pictures of things to send to your colleagues. Humanity depends on it!

A **note about the "notes"**[1] I learned during my doctoral program that, as scholar-practitioners, we are standing on the shoulders of giants. All of these ideas have been inspired by so many authors and trusted voices from my experiences in education. In order to honor their work, you will see the use of superscripts with direct quotes or other references to specific works. All of these notes are itemized by chapter at the end of the book, before the complete list of references.

Introduction

....

....

....

....

....

....

....

....

....

....

....

....

....

....

....

....

....

....

....

Hone Compassion

Hone Compassion

Hone Compassion: Leaders who take a H.U.M.A.N. approach are culturally competent, compassionate, and connected. Their compassion is expressed in their wholehearted approach to leadership and life, as they deeply strive to understand those within their spheres of influence.

- I consider myself a "servant leader." I believe my main contributions are in support of the growth of others.

- I strive to understand the worldview of others while continuing to uncover my own.

- I take action to help others move through painful situations.

- I practice deep listening. I am fully present when I engage with others.

- I seek to empower others by using the means available to me.

"Compassion is the daily practice of recognizing and accepting our shared humanity so that we treat ourselves and others with loving-kindness. And we take action in the face of suffering."

~Brené Brown

Key Concepts and Definitions

Hone: To refine or sharpen.

Compassion vs. Empathy: The key difference here is taking action. It's more than just "stepping in someone else's shoes;" it involves helping others to walk in them, too.

Cultural proficiency: Randall Lindsey's team's[1] definition is: *"esteeming culture, knowing how to learn about individual and organizational culture, and interacting effectively in a variety of cultural environments."* To be culturally proficient, then, leaders must truly understand those they serve, on the most human level.

Wholehearted: Brené Brown's term for a *"fully examined emotional life and a liberated heart, one that is free and vulnerable enough to love and be loved."*[2]

Servant leader: Relationship-driven leaders with a strong commitment to the growth and development of their people.

Worldview: The lenses through which we understand and interact with the world. Our childhood experiences and identity markers play a significant role in this.

Before you begin:

What draws you to this element today?

What situations are happening in your professional practice that need support from this element of the framework? What guidance are you hoping for today?

Record your thoughts in the space below. Notice how they change over time as you return to this element.

Date	Notes

Coaching Session 1

Coach: So, what's the most important thing for us to talk about today?

School Leader: I've been thinking a lot about the idea of "transaction" versus true "connection."

Coach: Say more about this.

School Leader: Well, it's about why people show up the way they do. Why do people come to school every day? I've been talking about this for a long time now…as a teacher, can you name what drives you to show up, every day? And "because it's easier than having a sub" or "it's part of the evaluation rubric" aren't the answers I'm looking for. I want my team to be all-in; I want them to want to be here because the work we do is important and meaningful. I want them to feel connected as human beings, not just to the lower-case 'w' work, but to the capital 'W' Work.

Coach: How are you helping them create these connections?

School Leader: That's just it; I'm not sure I am. I try to be as supportive as possible in my role, and empowering my team is really important to me. Sometimes, though, I feel like I am falling short. I really identify as a "servant leader," and I aim to truly empathize with my teachers in order to help them feel seen and valued. But it doesn't seem to be enough.

Coach: What would you want to see and hear on your team to let you know you ARE doing enough?

School Leader: Great question…I think I would see and hear a tangible level of compassion.

Coach: What do you mean by a "tangible level of compassion?"

School Leader: I read that the difference between empathy and compassion was action.[3] I'd like to see more people stepping up to support each other. I want to be able to feel that people care about one another; I want us all to find and experience joy in our work on a daily basis.

Coach: Sounds like an amazing culture to be a part of. And because you have such a clear vision around this, that tells me that some of these things are most likely already in place...I want you to tell me three different areas where you and others are experiencing joy and connection, and then let's see how we might multiply those.

School Leader: (takes a deep breath). Ok...I feel that sense of connection when our teacher leaders are facilitating small group discussions. I think people really respond well to them.

Coach: That's one...

School Leader: I love that we are becoming more comfortable with peer observations. There is still some apprehension from some, but we're getting better.

Coach: Peer observations are a wonderful way to build empathy! Ok, one more...

School Leader: At the beginning of the year, you and I talked about meeting one-on-one with each member of my faculty. I didn't think I would have time and space to do it, but I kept at it, and though it took me the entire month of September, I got to meet with everyone. That was a really powerful experience for me.

Coach: Ok! Would you be interested in talking about how to scale up these three things to help increase the connectivity on your team?

School Leader: Yes! I'm in.

Analysis

In the work of leading schools and districts, it is so easy to get caught up in the day-to-day tasks that require immediate attention to keep the school running. Throw in an angry phone call, a fistfight at lunch, or an unscheduled lockdown, and a school leader's day can turn into a constant melee of fires to put out. In this session, though, we see how an intentional focus on creating opportunities for compassionate connection on our teams can have a huge impact. By flexing our compassion muscles, we have the opportunity to deepen our understanding of others' experiences, thereby broadening our perspectives, which is central to our development as adults. Consider the state of the adult culture at your school: what is the level of engagement like? Is it one of compliance, in which people only participate because it is required? Or is there a real sense of connection through which people show up for each other because it matters? As a leader, how might your daily compassionate practices help enhance the sense of interrelatedness that people feel in their work and with each other?

Reflections In The Research

Many researchers and scholars agree on the importance of leaders being culturally proficient, compassionate, and connected. These attributes demonstrate a commitment to our shared humanity. Leaders can express their compassion in their wholehearted approach to leadership and life, as they sincerely strive to understand those within their spheres of influence. Brené Brown[4] reminds us that compassion should be a daily practice. This daily practice allows leaders to hone, or refine and develop, their compassion muscles. Through compassion, individuals can connect in deep and meaningful ways.

In a review of the literature regarding the meaning of compassion, researchers Strauss et al. compared multiple definitions. Their results synthesized a new definition of compassion, which describes it as a "cognitive, affective, and behavioral process."[3] Ultimately, the difference between compassion and empathy is a commitment to action. Brené Brown adds to this by noting that "empathy is a skill set that is one of the most powerful tools of compassion."[4] Empathy can be debilitating at times, though, as one becomes enveloped in another's pain.[5] As compassionate leaders in education, it is imperative to both recognize the multi-faceted nature of an individual's experience and be able to offer helpful tools to use on their journeys.

As adults in general and leaders, in particular, continue to develop, they gain a deeper understanding of those they work with.[6] For Simon Sinek, this means studying one's rivals, an element of his *Infinite Game*.[7] When one seeks out and embraces alternate points of view, studying how those different from them engage with their work can "challenge us, inspire us or force us to improve,"[7] all while helping leaders to understand the fuller picture of their work environments.[8] Most books on this topic embrace a strengths-based perspective, emphasizing respecting one another to cultivate positive emotions. These positive emotions build people's inherent aspirations and emphasize their teams' collective good. This calls for more emotionally intelligent leaders with a "servant's heart"[9] who recognize that power given away freely is an incredible gift.[10] These descriptions align with Randall Lindsey and colleagues' five behaviors of a culturally proficient professional. These are individuals who assess culture, value diversity, manage the dynamics of difference, adapt to diversity, and institutionalize cultural knowledge.[1] One way to operationalize these concepts is through the skill of listening.

Otto Scharmer, author of *Theory U*,[11] offers the technique of deep, generative listening to support leaders in their quest to hone their compassion. This process requires a purposeful shift in how leaders present themselves to others. According to Scharmer, "changing how you listen means that you change how you experience relationships and the world." Deep, generative listening helps build one's empathy and deconstructs the one-sided, presumptive stories one may be internalizing. "Hearing and helping others feel heard" is the first skill detailed in Dr. Jennifer Nash's Human Leadership Framework.[12] Leanne Holdsworth, Naryan Wong, and friends extend this idea, recognizing that "allowing people to be known as a whole person also communicates care."[13] Too often in schools, there is not enough time in the day to wholeheartedly listen to other adults amidst the frenzied rush to complete every required task. Nevertheless, everyone deserves the opportunity to participate in a conversation that allows them to be heard, seen, and validated. These are the compassionate moments that add to an individual's stores of trust and resilience, which will be discussed in the following chapters. When educational leaders model these behaviors for their teachers, they can encourage a shift of the adult cultures in their schools towards one that honors and elevates an individual's humanity.

Reflection Questions / Journal Prompts

What connections are you making to the coaching session?

How do you "operationalize compassion" on your team?

In your workplace, where do you see moments of genuine connection for people? How might you multiply these?

Considering all of this, who do you want to be, next?

5 Protocols and Practices for Developing Yourself

1) *Are You Listening?*

Many of us have heard some rendition of Steven Covey's famous line, *"Most people do not listen with the intent to understand; they listen with the intent to reply."* Far too often, we fall into the earlier category; our "listening" is actually just waiting for the other person to stop talking so we can share what we are thinking! One way to hone our compassion is to change the way we listen. Otto Scharmer, author of *Theory U*,[11] has identified 4 types of listening. These are:

Downloading: This type of listening is limited to reconfirming what we already know. Nothing new penetrates our bubble. This is the pretend listening so many of us do as we are waiting for our turn to talk.

Factual listening: We let the data talk to us and notice information that might be different from our current assumptions. Doing this requires opening the mind— that is, the capacity to suspend our habits of judgment. Here, we begin to be truly open to what the other person is saying.

Empathic listening: We see the situation through the eyes of another. Doing this requires opening the heart: using our feelings and our heart as an organ of tuning into another person's view. This is about trying to embrace the other person's perspective. Are we able to hear our way into understanding?

Generative listening: We listen for the highest future possibility to show up while holding a space for something new to be born. In his book, *Cultures of Thinking In Action*, Ron Ritchhart[14] reminds us to listen to our students for evidence of how they are thinking and engaging with the experiences in our classrooms. It's an equally powerful practice with adults.

As you "hone your compassion," pay attention to how you are listening to your teammates. Are you engaging in a "hallway conversation" while trying to listen but actually monitoring student

> "When we are listened to, it creates us, makes us unfold and expand. Ideas actually begin to grow within us and come to life."
>
> ~*The Arbinger Institute*

behavior? Or are you "just finishing up an email" and encouraging the other person to go on with their story? Being present is the first step to actually listening. Making changes to how you are listening is a great way to hone your compassion.

2) *Listening Set Asides*

Continuing with the idea of how we listen, there are a few other traps we fall into when we are listening. Cognitive Coaching,[15] as presented by The Thinking Collaborative, shares three practices we need to "set aside" if we are going to truly listen to another person. I have summarized them here. Which of these patterns do you tend to fall into?

Autobiographical listening: Here, we THINK we are connecting with the other person, when in fact, we have just made everything about us. Here's a scenario:

Colleague: "Uff...that was a really tough class. Everything I had planned totally fell apart, and that fire drill in the middle didn't help. I couldn't get back on track, and now I feel like I have to re-do everything I had planned for the rest of the week.

You: "I'm so sorry. I totally get it. The same thing happened to me yesterday, only it wasn't a fire drill, it was the unexpected play practice that took half of my kids! I mean, you think we could get some advance notice, right? So I spent my entire planning period tracking down kids to get them the updated info they need for their projects...

Sound familiar? A simple, "tell me more" could have changed our colleague's day, and instead, now we've put our colleague in the position of supporting us!

"Emotionally intelligent leaders have a servant's heart and are able to satisfy their own needs and wants while also serving the needs and wants of those they lead. Our ability to form deep, lasting connections with people separates us as leaders."

~Christopher Connors

Inquisitive listening: This is the pattern of asking for juicy details that aren't really relevant to the situation but satisfy our own curiosity. When a colleague needs to talk, we need to make sure we are focusing on the teller of the story, not asking questions that could be construed as a search for gossip (no matter how desperately you may want to know!).

Solution listening: There are times when a colleague may come to you for support, and they may explicitly ask you for advice. However, when we jump in with trying to solve all their problems with the way WE would handle a situation, we take away the other person's ability for self-actualization.

Keep these ideas in mind the next time a colleague comes to you with something to share. You might be surprised by the results!

3) How Empathetic Are You?

Want some insights into your own levels of empathy?

The Greater Good Science Center[16] at the University of California, Berkeley, is a wealth of information and resources. According to its mission statement, "The Greater Good Science Center studies the psychology, sociology, and neuroscience of well-being and teaches skills that foster a thriving, resilient, and compassionate society."

The Greater Good Science Center also has a whole section dedicated to supporting our schools: *Greater Good in Education: Science Based Practices for Kinder, Happier Schools.* Visit their website for information on student and adult well-being, building relationships, and so much more!

Their researchers have developed a questionnaire that will help determine just how empathetic you are. Head to this site to take the quiz and gain some new insights into who you are and how that might impact those around you:

https://greatergood.berkeley.edu/quizzes/take_quiz/empathy

(This quiz originally appeared on <u>Greater Good</u>, the online magazine of the Greater Good Science Center at UC Berkeley)

"Love and compassion are necessities, not luxuries. Without them, humanity cannot survive."

~Dalai Lama

4) Are You Putting People In Boxes?

Have you ever been having a conversation with a colleague, and they reveal something about themselves that makes you say, "REALLY! I had no idea!" That reaction is an indication that you might be putting someone into a box they don't belong in.

Somehow, many of us feel that we have a complete picture of our colleagues based on just a few details they feel comfortable sharing during an ice breaker at a faculty meeting. Without even realizing it, we prejudge and create entire narratives in our heads about who someone is based on those random pieces of information that never convey the whole story.

Ask yourself: who do you need to learn more about? How might you employ some of the different types of listening shared in this chapter to get a fuller sense of the human beings you work with?

Here's a challenge: make it a point to learn something new about every person you work with. Depending on the size of your staff or district, this might be an annual challenge or it could be monthly. The next section of this element has some additional

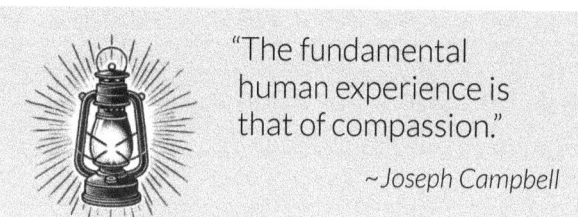

"The fundamental human experience is that of compassion."

~Joseph Campbell

ideas to help you operationalize this idea, but right now, I invite you to take a good look at the stories you might be telling yourself about your colleagues. Authentic connections will allow you to truly hone your compassion.

5) If These Walls Could Talk: Individual Practice

In schools, we spend a lot of time observing the interactions between the people. As an instructional coach, I have tracked questions that are asked and answered, monitored rates of engagement, and tallied who is doing most of the talking. But what does the physical environment say that can help us hone our compassion? Oftentimes, we become so used to the way things are, physically, that we stop paying attention to the impact they are having on our environment. Are we communicating that people are welcome? Or does the layout of furniture present unintended barriers? What about the signage? Is it all, "Don't"s and "No"s? Or are our hallways full of positive messages that invite people into our spaces? The environments we live and work in can have serious repercussions on our physical and mental well-being. Knowing this can help us better understand how these impacts manifest themselves in behaviors and attitudes.

Here's one way to focus on what messages your space is sending. (Note: this process is inspired by the *National School Reform Faculty's Ghost Visit*[17] protocol. You can find the complete steps and additional guidance for their protocol at https://nsrfharmony.org)

- Choose a time when the kids and teachers are not present.
- Wander the halls with the intention of answering this question: What are the walls saying in regard to who is welcome in your school?
- Look for evidence of:
  - Lighting and colors
  - Furniture placement/clutter
  - Items in need of repair or replacement
  - Signage and messaging
  - Anything else you might see that will give you insight into how people are showing up!
- If you can, try to continue viewing your physical space through this lens. What needs to change? What can be enhanced?

"The real voyage of discovery consists not in seeking new landscapes but in having new eyes."

~Marcel Proust

5 Protocols and Practices for Developing Your Team

1) 1:1 Meetings

In the corporate world, one-on-one meetings between managers and employees are a highly valued experience. According to a study published in the *Harvard Business Review*:[18]

> ***One-on-ones remain vital.*** *We can quantify actual time managers spent in one-on-one meetings with direct reports based on calendared meeting invitations. In the companies we analyzed, the average manager spent 30 minutes every 3 weeks with each of their employees. Perhaps unsurprisingly, employees who got little to no one-on-one time with their manager were more likely to be disengaged. On the flip side, those who get twice the number of one-on-ones with their manager relative to their peers are 67% less likely to be disengaged.*

I have been recommending this practice to school leaders for years. And I get it; trying to find the time among the latest state mandates, the student waiting to talk to you, and the teacher who unexpectedly is going to be out for a week is difficult. But the payoff is too good to pass up.

If you are willing to try these, here are a few key things to remember:

- 1:1 meetings are NOT about evaluation. They are about connection.

- 1:1 meetings need to be as sacred as possible. We know life gets in the way at school, but do your best to honor these meetings.

- 1:1 meetings are also a time for your team to learn about you; but remember, don't make it ALL about you. *(see Listening Set Asides in the previous section)*

- Take notes so you can follow up and keep the conversation alive.

If you are fortunate enough to have instructional coaches in your school or district, they can also support with more regular contact with your teachers. But as the leader in your school or district, I can't stress enough how important these conversations are for you to have, personally.

A few variations:

BOY (Beginning Of The Year) Conversations

As the leader, schedule a 15-minute meeting with everyone in your building. Yes, EVERYONE. The person who left at the end of the last school year is not the person who has returned this year. Check in. Find out how things are going. Let them know you are there, and you care. Use these three questions to guide your meeting:

- What was a highlight of your break?
- What are you most looking forward to this school year?
- What can I do as a leader to help you be successful this year?

Leadership Team 1:1s

If you lead a district team of building leaders or a building team of assistant principals or other directors, have regular check-ins with each individual outside of your team meetings. (If your team works with a leadership coach, even better! But you can still connect with your team on how things are going.) Use these three simple questions to guide your meetings:

- What is really going well for you right now?
- What is something that is taking up too much of your time right now?
- What can I do to help things be better?

> "Remind them they're worthy. Tell them they're incredible. Be a light in a too often dim world."
>
> ~Unknown

2) The Compliment Sandwich

So many of us were trained that when we have to give feedback that isn't easy or positive, it seems so much better served in the traditional "compliment sandwich." Picture this:

Slice of bread: A genuine compliment about the person you are speaking with.
It is so clear to see how much you care about your kids!

Sandwich insides: The "constructive" criticism
And sometimes, I see them taking just a little advantage of how much you care about them through behavior that isn't always respectful.

Slice of bread: Another genuine compliment to soften the blow.
But your classroom is looking great this year!

What does the teacher hear? *My classroom management is terrible. And apparently, you hated my classroom set up last year.*

We've all been there. And that sandwich is never tasty. Organizational psychologist Roger Schwartz[19] explains it this way:

> *Imagine telling the people your strategy [for the compliment sandwich]. You would say something like, "Alex and Stacey, I have some negative feedback to give you. I'll start with some positive feedback to relax you, and then give you the negative feedback, which is the real purpose of our meeting. I'll end with more positive feedback so you won't be so disappointed or angry at me when you leave my office. How does that work for you?*

Organizational Psychologist Adam Grant has shared these research-proven 19 words to help people be more open to feedback: "I'm giving you these comments because I have very high expectations and I know that you can reach them."[20] (You can also listen to a podcast[21] with Adam Grant and Jennifer Garner talking about this very topic! You can find it on https://adamgrant.net/podcasts)

"I'm giving you these comments because I have very high expectations and I know that you can reach them."

~David Yeager, et al.

Think about how this language might be received by the teachers on your teams. It's a compassionate way to help people continue to grow in their instructional and professional practices that communicates both care and support.

3) *The Filters Through Which We See the World*

Our "worldviews" are the filters through which we understand and interact with the world. Our childhood experiences and identity markers play a significant role in these, as they contribute to how much social capital and power we have in a given situation.

Take a moment and consider the following:

- Your age / Affiliate generation (Baby Boomer, X, Millennial, Z)
- Your assigned gender at birth vs. the gender you embody now
- Your race
- Your religion
- Your ethnicity
- Your marital status
- The makeup of your current family
- Your parents' marital status
- Your family members / your role in the family you grew up in
- Your level of education
- Your financial status as a child vs. your financial status now
- Where you grew up and what that means to you
- Your physical or neuro-differences
- Your physical size
- Where you work vs. where your parents work
- Opportunities you have had for travel or cultural exchange

I have done this activity using actual coffee filters. Here's how:

- Each team member gets a coffee filter.

- People write a word or two for each bullet point.

- Once all are accounted for, ask people to think about the ones (5-6) that have the strongest pull for them. Write those words again.

- Take another look. Of those 5-6, which ones are the most important for you? Write those words as many times as you feel it takes to represent their importance.

- For example, if being a woman is the marker you identify with the most, you might write that word another 5 times. Then, if your religion is the second strongest marker for you, you might write that word another 4 times.

At the end, people have a coffee filter covered with words that represent how they experience and make meaning of the world around them. The words that are written the most indicate the "filters" they use to process information and make decisions about a course of action.

"The greatest tragedy for any human being is going through their entire lives believing the only perspective that matters is their own."

~Doug Baldwin

Connecting back to our development as adults, ask your team: How has your filter changed over time? What words have become smaller or less important? What new words have you added?

4) Kindness Partners

I have to admit I am not a fan of any events during the holiday season that involve drawing names and secretly giving gifts to people. Personally, I feel like it is just one more unnecessary stress to spend money on things that people might not necessarily want or need, just to be a part of the group. For me, it falls into the category of "forced fun and structured silliness." I don't like it. And I feel better now that my feelings are out there!

If we truly want to hone our compassion, why not be kind to each other all year? What if you had an "annual kindness campaign," with quarterly "kindness partners"? Here's how it might work:

- Each quarter, your teammates draw the name of one person they will secretly support.

- Each week, the Kindness Partner does something free or free-ish for their person to let them know they are seen and valued.

  - Free-ish could be less than $5.

- Here are some ideas:

  - Handwritten notes with compliments on something that the partner observed that week.

  - A Monday morning motivational message.

  - A mid-week pick-me-up coffee or favorite snack, delivered by someone else, who will then also benefit from the joy of the recipient's reaction.

  - A handwritten note sharing something you read or heard that reminds you of the person.

- At the end of the pre-determined time period, there is a small "reveal" celebration. Thank yous are shared all around, and new names are drawn.

- If you have time, ask the givers to share something they learned about their partner. This is another way to help individuals feel seen and heard.

- This allows the "holiday spirit" to be part of every day. It hones our compassion as we start to see our kindness partners in a different, perhaps more meaningful way.

> "One of the secrets of life is that all that is really worth doing is what we do for others."
>
> ~Lewis Carroll

5) *If These Walls Could Talk: Teams Edition*

Completing a silent observation is even more powerful when you can compare notes with your team. This is a fantastic way to help understand what others are thinking, as well as an opportunity to see things through someone else's eyes. As a reminder, here is some background on this process:

> *In schools, we spend a lot of time observing the interactions between the people. But what does the physical environment say that can help us hone our compassion? Oftentimes, we become so used to the way things are, physically, that we stop paying attention to the impact they are having on our environment. Are we communicating that people are welcome? Or does the layout of furniture present unintended barriers? What about the signage? Is it all, "Don't"s and "No"s? Or are your hallways full of positive messages that invite people into your spaces? The environments we live and work in can have serious repercussions on our physical and mental well-being. Understanding this can help you better understand how these impacts manifest themselves in behaviors and attitudes.*

(Note: this process is inspired by *National School Reform Faculty's Ghost Visit*[17] protocol. You can find the complete steps and additional guidance for their protocol at https://nsrfharmony.org)

Choose a time when the kids and teachers are not present.

- As a team, determine your focus. What will help you understand how the physical space is impacting your teammates? Some possible ideas are:
  - Lighting and colors
  - Furniture placement/clutter
  - Items in need of repair or replacement
  - Signage and messaging

Spend 10-15 minutes wandering your halls, and peering into classrooms. Take notes that align with your determined focus.

- Remember to observe silently. Take notes, but save the discussion for the debrief.

The Debrief

- As you share your observations, remember to consider the action steps that will follow.

- One possible protocol to debrief would be the "See-Think-Wonder" routine from Project Zero[22]:

    Step 1: Make a list: What did participants physically see in the areas you collectively identified?

    Step 2: Based on what you saw, what do you think about the messages the physical space is sending? What inferences can you make?

    Step 3: Considering these thoughts and inferences, what new ideas do you have? What do you wonder about that might help enhance or strengthen the physical spaces to be more welcoming and inclusive for everyone?

"It's not what you look at that matters. It's what you see."

-Henry David Thoreau

5 Resources To Keep You Learning And Growing

Atlas of the Heart is a beautiful book that explores 87 emotions found in the human experience. Brown's work is incredibly inspiring and helps build connections between us all.

"The real job of a leader isn't being in charge, it's about taking care of those in our charge." ~Simon Sinek.[23] On YouTube, search for "Simon Sinek Empathy" to watch Simon Sinek explain the importance of empathy for leaders.

Famed organizational experts, Lee Bolman and Terrence Deal, offer a parable to help leaders understand four gifts of leadership: love, power, authorship, and significance. Understanding these gifts will help you become more compassionate in your interactions.

David Cooperrider is considered the leading expert in the field of Appreciative Inquiry. This is one resource to learn more about this practice. You can learn more about Dr. Cooperrider and his work via the Fowler Center for Business as an Agent of World Benefit at Case Western University.

The Book of Joy with His Holiness the Dalai Lama and Archbishop Desmond Tutu is a masterclass in compassion. While centered on joy, this is a remarkable treasure to help us answer the question, "How do we find joy in the face of life's inevitable suffering?

Hone Compassion: Key Takeaways

The difference between "compassion" and "empathy" is action.

Compassion is a skill that needs to be practiced and refined, every day.

Find the time to get to know the stories of those people around you. Learn about the "whole adult" to deepen your understanding of how your team is working

---

Understand One's Identity As A Leader

Understand One's Identity As A Leader

Understand One's Identity As A Leader: Leaders who take a H.U.M.A.N. approach are aware of their strengths and opportunities for growth. They courageously and intentionally model reflection and change.

- I am clear about the values that guide me, and I allow others to be guided by their values. I recognize and celebrate they may be different from my own.

- I have a strong sense of self. I understand the potential of my capabilities and know where I have room to grow.

- I understand the impact of cultural factors on my identity, and I bring this awareness to creating a culture of inclusion that enhances the feelings of belonging.

- I consistently seek out ways to learn about the world around me. I set goals for myself to continue improving in a variety of areas.

- I recognize when my behaviors or thoughts indicate I may be out of alignment with my values, and I do what I must to realign.

"As you navigate through the rest of your life, be open to collaboration. Other people and other people's ideas are often better than your own. Find a group of people who challenge and inspire you. Spend a lot of time with them, and it will change your life."

~Amy Poehler

Key Concepts and Definitions

Identity: The fact of being who or what a person or thing is.

Values: A person's principles or standards of behavior; one's judgment of what is important in life.

Cultural factors: Race, ethnicity, gender, religion, age, geography, etc. that contribute to one's sense of self as well as power and privilege in society.

Before you begin:

What draws you to this element today?

What situations are happening in your professional practice that need support from this element of the framework? What guidance are you hoping for today?

Record your thoughts in the space below. Notice how they change over time as you return to this element.

Date	Notes

Coaching Session 2

Coach: So, what's the most important thing for us to talk about today?

School Leader: I am really struggling. At the district leadership team meeting the other day, I could not hide my emotions. I feel like I am functioning—barely—with a constant level of frustration. I've been snappy with everyone. This is NOT who I am. I've been reflecting a lot about the idea we talked about last time: connection versus transaction. Connection is one of my values, but I feel so out of alignment these days.

Coach: Tell me more about this. What are some specific things that make you feel disconnected?

School Leader: I just feel like…I'm totally alone. I can see the path forward, but we get so caught up in the status quo, in the way we've always done things, and no one wants to try something new. Like, just the other day, I sent an email to the team with this idea I had to address our attendance problem, and I got a very dismissive email response—reply all, mind you—saying how it would never work, blah blah blah. I had to work really hard not to fire off an email back, which upsets me even more, because I am NOT the person who gets angry and reacts. But I find myself in these situations way too often, and the moments feel closer together…like the walls are closing in.

Coach: This is causing you real pain. Twice you've said the words, "This is not who I am." What steps have you taken to re-align with your values?

School Leader: I'm doing all of the things…I have my gratitude practice, I'm exercising and making sure I'm eating right; I am getting outside…

Coach: So you are using the practices that have helped you in the past. Why do you think those things are not working for you now, if they had worked in the past?

School Leader: I'm not sure…everything just seems to be so much harder now.

Coach: Say more about that.

School Leader: I just...I just feel like I don't recognize myself anymore. I don't like who I am...who this role needs me to be.

Coach: So, how might you reconnect with your values and regain your sense of self?

School Leader: I don't know.

Coach: ....

School Leader: Ok, ok. I can monitor the voice in my head, and remember my go-to question of "Tell me more" when someone says something ridiculous...

Coach: (clears throat)

School Leader: ...when someone says something I don't agree with. I need to remember to lean in as opposed to pulling back—which I know is totally one of my self-protective strategies; the more distance I keep, the safer I remain.

Coach: How does it feel when you retreat?

School Leader: It just makes me question everything.

Coach: So? What are we going to do? Are you willing to try to find "connection" again?

School Leader: I think so.

Coach: Ok, good. Because it has to start with connecting to yourself, first, which I think we are starting to do here. When you feel connected to your truth—when you are truly being your authentic self—you can start to embrace the perspectives of others and build connections again.

Analysis

Have you felt this way before? That feeling of being so out of alignment you don't even like yourself? Don't worry, this is NOT a permanent state! On our journeys of becoming the best versions of ourselves, there will be moments—or perhaps considerably longer periods—when we revert to negative behaviors that are far from matching the self we want to present to the world. As described in the introduction, in the world of adult development, this is referred to as a state of "fallback." When we are triggered, we take on behaviors and revert to ways of making sense of the world that protect the self we have created, but those behaviors only keep us trapped in the place we don't want to be.

But, there is hope! According to Valerie Livesay[1]:

> *Fallback, when we recognize and accept it, can be about understanding when and why we are not able to bring our better self; about reframing our expectations of who we are in this world; about accepting the full messiness that is an inevitable component of being human; about coming to know and love a more authentic version of self; and about cultivating the environments for others to do the same.*

Working with your coach can help you move through these moments to help bring you back into alignment with wherever you are on your journey of development. This all starts with knowing who you are, what values are guiding you at this moment, and most importantly, paying attention to the warning signs that things are heading in the wrong direction. A coaching conversation is a great way to reconnect with your best self.

"There is always light if we are brave enough to see it. There is always light if we are brave enough to be it."

~Amanda Gorman

Reflections In The Research

So much has been written detailing the superpower that is being aware of your strengths and opportunities for growth. These are key elements of the H.U.M.A.N. approach to educational leadership. The literature shows that within this awareness is the courageous and intentional practice of modeling reflection to bring about change. And so, transforming schools starts with their leaders and the emotionally intelligent act of looking inward. This type of reflection helps leaders recognize that deep and lasting change begins with an understanding of their relationships with the systems they are a part of.[2,3,4]

Through their 40 years of research on leadership, *The Leadership Challenge* authors Jim Kouzes and Barry Posner have identified that "when you understand who you are and what you believe, you can act with integrity when giving voice to those values."[5] It is an act of courage to identify your struggles and successes and to be open to welcoming new perspectives while entertaining ideas that are different from your own.[6,7,8,9,10,11] This state of reflection also requires a level of cultural proficiency, which Randall Lindsey et al. defined as "esteeming culture, knowing how to learn about individual and organizational culture, and interacting effectively in a variety of cultural environments."[12] This understanding will require a commitment to listening and acting upon new information in ways that acknowledge and celebrate the uniqueness of each teacher in the community of your school.

Leadership coaches Bob and Megan Tschannen-Moran add that this way of leading will require "new conversations [that] generate new truths and new possibilities,"[13] which supports one's development as an adult. Ellie Drago-Severson notes that "self-transforming knowers experience a new sense of freedom to express the self and let others be themselves."[7] In turn, these conversations and this newfound sense of freedom might help the individual members of the adult cultures of your schools become better at learning and "better at life,"[2] as expressed by author and researcher Michael Fullan. When leaders do this internal work, they can support those in their spheres of influence to take steps toward their own development and personal transformations. This is part of the H.U.M.A.N. approach to encourage positive and professional shifts within our collective communities, and ultimately, a better humanity.

Reflection Questions / Journal Prompts

What connections are you making to the coaching session?

What are your two core values?

What behaviors do you exhibit when you are out of alignment with your core values? What does "fallback" look like for you?

What steps do you take (or will you take) when you recognize your own warning signs?

Which cultural factors are most important to you and how you see the world?

How often do you take time for intentional reflection? What kind of practice do you use?

Considering all this, who do you want to be, next?

....

....

....

....

....

....

....

....

5 Protocols and Practices for Developing Yourself

1) Determining Your Core Values

Quick! Can you name your school or district's core values?

If you you rattled them off with ease, congratulations! That is evidence that you are in the right place in your professional career! The values have been ingrained in you, and hopefully, you are also living them out loud.

If you struggled…don't worry. You are not alone. But the first step to connecting with your school or district's values is to make sure you are clear on your own.

Our "core values" can be defined as a fundamental set of beliefs or principles that guide our actions. It is possible that you might be rushing through your days without a conscious awareness of what your values are or how they affect you. Sometimes, this applies to our schools, too. Most districts list their core values on their website; 5-7 seems to be a pretty common number. Hopefully, these values are front and center for all of the work you do. You revisit them at the start of a faculty meeting, or maybe your professional development plan references how the intentional scope and sequence brings these values to life.

Or, it has been known to happen that a list of values was generated years ago by a various group of well-meaning stakeholders representing school employees, students, families, and local business owners. They undoubtedly went through a thorough process like the one I'll describe next. Five values were determined, and they have been immortalized on the district's website ever since. Mission accomplished!

Then, a few years later, someone shows up for an interview and makes a connection to the district's values. Around the table, there are blank faces as folks on the interview team try to remember what those values are….

It is essential that whatever your district's process for determining its values, you are clear on your own. In a perfect world, your values will also align with what your school or district has also selected. If they don't, it might be time to reconsider your work environment.

The internet is full of all sorts of resources for defining your core values. The basic idea, though, is to really think about what is MOST central to your entire being.

- Many protocols you find move through some kind of elimination practice, such as this:
    - Start by reviewing a lengthy list of values to help generate your thinking.
    - *Round 1: circle everything that is important to you*
    - *Round 2: narrow all of those you circled down to 10*
    - *Round 3: narrow the list to 5.*
        - I really like Brené Brown's[14] suggestion to narrow the list down further to two. These are truly representative of your core.
- As you grow and develop and experience more of the world and life itself, it's ok if your values shift over time. That's all part of our journeys of living out loud the highest expression of our adult selves.
- At this moment, my two core values are "compassion" and "connection." "Trust" is also in there, but that, for me, is part of connection. There are lots of people with their curated lists out there; it doesn't matter which one you use. The point is that you spend some time uncovering what are the two driving forces in your life. Then, this new self-awareness can help you recognize when you are out of alignment with those two values. With time, this becomes easier and easier.

> "Your beliefs become your thoughts,
> your thoughts become your words,
> your words become your actions,
> your actions become your habits,
> your habits become your values,
> your values become your destiny."
>
> ~Mahatma Gandhi

2) *"Fix Your Face"*

When we are out of alignment with our values or are feeling attacked in some way at school, we can "fallback" into some pretty negative behaviors in order to protect ourselves.

My first inclination that something is wrong? I start to notice what needs to be cleaned or organized.

"Why are the chairs not perfectly aligned at the table?"
"Can't anyone else hear the laundry buzzer?"
"Don't worry (dripping with sarcasm), I'll do the dishes AGAIN…"

These are the warning lights. Next thing you know, I'm huffing and puffing, and somehow everything I look at is a mess…and that is a clue for me to take a walk.

I also need to remember that all of my emotions are easily read on my face. This is where "fix your face" comes into play. I wrote this on a sticky note once to remind myself to be more open and less judgmental.

I invite you to use the journal pages at the end of this chapter to consider your "warning lights." What behaviors let you know you are out of alignment with your values or are feeling triggered in some other way?

Here's the good news: when we can recognize these behaviors in ourselves, we can change them. They might be scary and painful to admit, but this is how we understand ourselves as leaders and begin to take a more H.U.M.A.N. approach.

"And the day came when the risk to remain tight in a bud was more painful than the risk it took to blossom"

~Anaïs Nin

3) *What Brings You Joy?: Individual Practice*

(I wish I had a source for this. I participated in this activity during a leadership training[15] many years ago; unfortunately, I do not know where it is from. But I love it, and I hope you will, too!)

Your challenge: Make 2 lists.

- The first list: 20 things that bring you joy.
- The second list: 20 things that you are good at.
- Here's the catch: you can't stop at 12, or 16, or 19.
  - **You need to identify 20 items on EACH LIST.**
- If you get stuck, ask your friends, ask your family, ask your pet.
- Then, take a look. Read it again, and a few more times after that. What do you notice? How has your thinking shifted about YOU from before writing this list to now? How might you use this information to reground when the school day / week / semester throws you off balance?

20 things that bring me joy:	20 things I'm good at:
1.	1.
2.	2.
3.	3.
4.	4.
5.	5.
6.	6.
7.	7.
8.	8.
9.	9.
10.	10.
11.	11.
12.	12.
13.	13.
14.	14.
15.	15.
16.	16.
17.	17.
18.	18.
19.	19.
20.	20.

4) Morning Routines

How your day starts can have a significant impact on everything that happens next. Planning an intentional, positive, and healthy beginning is a game changer. I have been working out in the morning for so many years that my day is actually WORSE when I skip the workout. I eat the same thing for breakfast. I prepare my lunches for the entire week on Sundays. I aim to turn the light out by 9pm. Might this be a little compulsive? Maybe. BUT, what it does is provide me with the consistency to be more efficient. James Clear talks a lot about routines and practices in his book, *Atomic Habits*. One of the most often quoted lines from this mecca of self-improvement strategies is, "You do not rise to the level of our goals. You fall to the level of your systems."[16] So, as you work to truly understand yourself and the conditions necessary for you to be your best for your team, what systems need to be in place for you to thrive? Do you have a specific morning or evening routine that helps you start or end the day?

Here's my morning routine:

- Wake up at 5am. (I try not to hit the 'snooze button' per Coach Ted Lasso's wisdom.)

- Repeat the sentence, "Today is going to be a GREAT day, because I GET to…."

    ◦ Notice the difference between "have to" and "get to." This positivity helps you control your narrative!

- Drink a full bottle of water. Hydration is key!

- I do check my email first thing. Some people are resistant to this idea, but it helps me feel better prepared - in the world of education, you never know what wacky thing may have happened in the night.

- Out the door to exercise by 5:30am.

    ◦ Yep—outside, as much as possible. Even in the winter, in the dark and cold. There are SOME mornings where I live when it is just too cold and icy. But that's why treadmills were invented!

    ◦ Whether it's running or walking, a minimum of 30 minutes has become a staple of my life.

- Follow the run or walk with 15-30 minutes of yoga (depending on what time that first meeting is).

- 2-5 minutes of breathing and positive affirmations.

- Eat a protein-filled breakfast: My "go-to" is hard-boiled eggs and avocado on toast.

- Prep my coffee with almond milk and a scoop of collagen powder and take it to go. (I'm a two-cups-a-day coffee drinker, but I feel like my morning beverage is really coffee-flavored almond milk as opposed to an IV of caffeine.)

- And off I go! My list is long, but it has been curated over time. If you don't have a morning routine yet, maybe choose one or two things to do consistently and see what happens!

"There's two buttons I never like to hit: That's panic and snooze."

~ Ted Lasso

5) Implicit Association Test (IAT)

As we work to understand our identity, it's important to peel the layers of the proverbial onion to begin to understand that which is not as obvious. Many of us think we are unbiased, good people. And yet, we all have so many unconscious biases we're not even aware of until we take a real, honest look. At least that's the way this process has been for me. Now, instead of beating myself up for having a bias, I can recognize it and say, "yep, there's another one…" and work to overcome it and be better because of this new awareness.

Interested to see what biases you might hold? The Implicit Association Test from Harvard *"measures attitudes and beliefs that people may be unwilling or unable to report. The IAT may be especially interesting if it shows that you have an implicit attitude that you did not know about."*

This test might reveal to you insights into relationships with people on your team, or provide more information that explains why certain patterns might be repeating themselves in your life. Ready to find out?

Go to https://implicit.harvard.edu/implicit/takeatest.html to take the test. Use your results as a springboard on your developmental journey.

"Do the best you can until you know better. Then when you know better, do better."

~Maya Angelou

5 Protocols and Practices for Developing Your Team

1) "Where I'm From" Poems

This is a classic exercise in uncovering significant aspects of our childhood that contribute to our identity as adults. There are a variety of templates on the Internet, but I love the original from George Ella Lyon. You can read more about George Ella Lyon and the "I am From" project that dates back to 1989 on her website: http://www.georgeellalyon.com/where.html

A powerful exercise for individuals, the details and insights revealed through writing these poems help team members make connections as they begin to understand just a little more about each other. You could add a poem writing session to your leadership team retreat, or maybe there could be time dedicated at each of your leadership meetings for a different member to share their creation. However you choose to use this, you will all walk away with a deeper understanding of yourself as well as those you work with.

Here is mine, following the original format provided by George Ella Lyon.

I am from jungle gyms,

From bologna and cheese sandwiches with Miracle Whip

From riding bikes

All day, hatching plans for wild adventures.

Freedom

I am from lightning bugs and helicopter seeds from Maple trees, and the cicadas that come once every 17 years.

I'm from Aunt Joanie's deviled eggs and boxes of chocolate-covered maraschino cherries

From Margie and Dennis and Linda

I'm from Sugar and Spice Softball in the suburbs and Cubs' games in the city

From hopping out of the car to see if the corn was knee-high by the 4th of July

From casseroles made with cream of anything soup.

I'm from not being baptized - the only one of 24 grandchildren;

From the garbage truck that took my brother's leg and the

The small town parades we continued to march in.

I'm from the albums of times before;

when we waited for the photos to be developed, revealing to us the truth of moments captured in an instant;

The magic of reality without editing.

2) Small Fires

"Small fires" is a term the fabulous team of instructional coaches I worked with once used to describe a seating format where participants are knee-to-knee; i.e. not around a table. Removing any physical barriers allows for deeper connection.

> This process is modeled after the Microlab, another one of the many protocols available on the National School Reform Faculty (NSRF) website (https://nsrfharmony.org). It allows small groups to go deep, quickly, and it also asks participants to be ok with silence. Here is how NSRF describes the purpose of their Microlab protocol:
>
> *The purpose of the Microlab protocol is to address a specific sequence of questions in a structured format with small groups, using active listening skills. The Microlab is useful for team-building and democratizing participation because it asks that participants equalize communication and withhold judgment. It affirms people's ideas and builds community while addressing specific content issues.*[17]
>
> You can find the step-by-step guidance as well as suggested questions on the NSRF website.

For this process, ask your participants to form a group of 3. Imagine there is a "small fire" between you, and you are huddled close together.

One unique (and sometimes, initially awkward) element of NSRF's Microlab is that each speaker gets the full, pre-determined talk time for themselves. The listeners do not interrupt, make connections, ask questions, or say anything during the speaker's designated time. This can be VERY challenging for some participants because we want to make sure the speaker feels seen and valued. But remind the listeners JUST to listen. If the speaker does not use their entire time, the group will sit quietly in reflection. Sometimes, the silence encourages the speaker to add more details. Sometimes, we just need to let the information sink in.

Remember to respect confidentiality throughout these situations. Consider employing the "Vegas Rule:" *What is said here, stays here; what is learned here, leaves here.* Additionally, this is not a place for venting, complaining, or gossiping. It's a moment for us to share what is in our hearts and connect to one another on a very human level.

Using this protocol with your team can increase connection while your understanding of each other grows. National School Reform Faculty offers a list of questions you might use. A few of my favorites (not on the list) to use with teams are:

- What were you like as a student at the grade level you teach/lead now?

- What are you most proud of, professionally, from the last year? What did this situation teach you about yourself?

- What is your educator superpower?

- What is the one gift you bring to the team that others need?

- What is one thing people need to know about working with you?

- What is one event, moment, or situation, that has had the most profound impact on you as an educator?

- If you had to give advice to your first-year teacher self, what would you say? Why?

"My humanity is bound up in yours. I am. Only because you are."

~Archbishop Desmond Tutu

3) What Brings You Joy?: Teams Edition

(As noted in the individual practice, I wish I had a source for this. I participated in this activity during a leadership training[15] many years ago, but I do not know where it is from. But I love it, and I hope you will, too!)

- The challenge is to make 2 lists.
- The first list: 20 things that bring you joy.
- The second list: 20 things that you are good at.
- Here's the catch: you can't stop at 12, or 16, or 19. You need to identify 20 items on EACH LIST.

- If you get stuck, ask your friends, ask your family, ask your pet.
- Then, with your team, read it out loud.
  - Your team's task is to listen deeply and share new insights they gain about you while listening to your lists. Maybe your list reveals what a truly caring and generous person you are. Or maybe your list demonstrates your passion for adventure. The reflection from your team is the illuminating part; you will hear some wonderful things about yourself, and your team will learn interesting things about each other!

20 things that bring me joy:	*20 things I'm good at:*
1.	1.
2.	2.
3.	3.
4.	4.
5.	5.
6.	6.
7.	7.
8.	8.
9.	9.
10.	10.
11.	11.
12.	12.
13.	13.
14.	14.
15.	15.
16.	16.
17.	17.
18.	18.
19.	19.
20.	20.

4) Team Questionnaire

When a new team comes together, it's important to take time to understand each other's work habits. For example, one teammate might have small children at home, and therefore only has some quiet time after 9pm when the little ones go to bed. Or, someone else might be up at 5am, sending emails before they head for a workout. You might also want to know about someone's preferences for text messages versus emails. And most importantly, it's always good to know what a teammate needs to keep them going when days are not so good. Here is a questionnaire I have used with new teams:

1) **Who and where are your people?** Do you live here solo, or are you here with family and pets?

2) **What are your work habits?** Are you a 'morning lark' or a 'night owl'? Planner or a Procrastinator? How do you prefer to communicate? Email? Text? Face-to-face?

3) Would you describe yourself as a **natural leader**? Or someone who prefers working **behind the scenes**?

4) What is your **go-to snack or a favorite treat** to get you through the day? Do you keep a stash of chocolate? Love a mid morning cup of coffee?

5) **What do you like to do** when you are not focused on school?

6) **How do you like to receive feedback?** Written? Face to face conversation?

7) **What do you need when you are NOT your best self?**

8) What is your **theme song?**

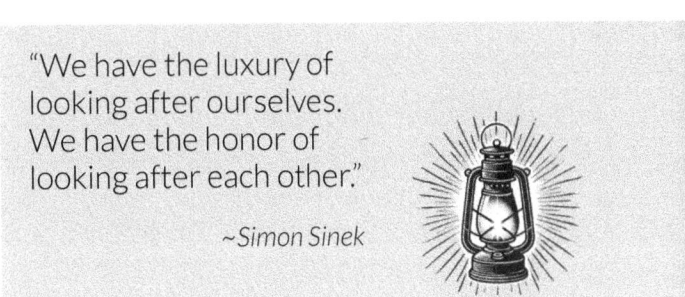

"We have the luxury of looking after ourselves. We have the honor of looking after each other."

~Simon Sinek

5) Personality Tests

I have to admit, I was pretty devastated when the author and researcher Adam Grant used a scientific study to counter my belief in astrology.[18] I love the spiritual connection that comes from thinking we are all bits of stardust from the Universe beyond time (I'm an Aries with Libra rising, for the record, and I personally feel those traits couldn't be more accurate). Regardless of your thoughts on astrology, there are several other personality tests that can give insights into who you are and how you show up on your team.

16 Personalities: This is based on the Myers-Briggs test and refers to 5 different personality aspects: Energy, Mind, Nature, Tactics and Identity. The 5th element, identity, has to do with our confidence and relationship with stress. And THEN - they give you an archetype, which makes it even more fun! (I'm an INFJ-A: The Advocate.) Find out your type at www.16personalites.com.

Enneagram: The Enneagram is an "emotionally focused system" with 9 different personality types. It explains different types of intelligence: heart, head, and body. There are several free tests available on the Internet!

True Colors: True Colors breaks your personality into 4 easy to identify categories, which the researchers have color-coded. Read about the research and the history of the assessment at www.truecolorsintl.com.

Love Languages: Though originally created to help couples communicate better, there is now a version for the workplace: *"This book helps supervisors and managers effectively communicate appreciation and encouragement to their employees, resulting in higher levels of job satisfaction, healthier relationships between managers and employees, and decreased cases of burnout."* I'm a gift giver (though others might call me a food pusher!). Discover your Love Language at www.5lovelanguages.com.

"I am large. I contain multitudes.

~Walt Whitman

5 Resources To Keep You Learning And Growing

As you continue to get better acquainted with yourself in order to take a more H.U.M.A.N. approach to your leadership, chapter one of Elena Aguilar's *Onward Workbook* has over 30 reflection activities to help you dive more deeply into who you are and why you are amazing. Check out the rest of her catalog, too!

Also grounded in adult development theory (and a total inspiration for this book), Jennifer Abrams's work *Stretching Your Learning Edges: Growing UP at Work* has a variety of exercises and self-assessments to help you develop as an individual and transform your school. The 'Know Your Identity Facet' aligns perfectly here.

Referenced above in the 'Morning Routines' section, James Clear's *Atomic Habits* and the weekly "3-2-1 Newsletter" has reached millions of individuals who are working to make lifestyle changes on the road to being their best selves.

From the creators of Stanford's D-School, *Designing Your Life*, by Bill Burnett and Dave Evans is a master class (literally!) on how to truly understand who you are and what you need to have the best life possible. I love the "Health-Work-Play-Love" dashboard. Check it out to start designing YOUR best life!

I first stumbled across Stephanie Harrison's daily newsletter of personal reminders for resilience and happiness, now there is a book, *New Happy!* The daily newsletter definitely lives up to its claim that it *"will help you be happier, achieve your goals, and find your purpose."* The daily artwork is beautiful and thought-provoking, and it makes my life better!

Understand One's Identity As A Leader: Key Takeaways

When we know our core values and are committed to keeping them at the forefront of all we do, we can be more intentional in our actions and decisions.

Recognizing the behaviors that indicate we are out of alignment with our core values is a key step to returning to alignment and moving out of fallback.

The more grounded we are in our own self-awareness and self-knowledge, the better we will be able to guide our teams on their own journeys.

Our identities are always in a state of flux: embrace who you are today, and be open to who you are becoming.

Make Meaning For Others
While Motivated By Vision

Make Meaning For Others While Motivated By A Vision

Make Meaning for Others While Motivated by a Vision: Leaders who take a H.U.M.A.N. approach are driven by an internal purpose that inspires others to make meaningful change.

- I can articulate what my purpose is, and I help others connect with theirs.

- I focus on the "big picture," and the reason why the work I do makes a difference.

- I support others to find meaning in their work by identifying connections they may not see yet.

- I bring an appreciative mindset to my work. I look for the good and find moments of joy.

- I believe I am a catalyst for change, and I want to bring others with me in this work.

> "The two most important days in life are the day you born and the day you find out why."
>
> ~Mark Twain

Key Concepts and Definitions

Mission vs. Vision: While often used interchangeably, they are not. A vision is the big picture goal, and the mission is the steps you or the team will take to get there. Missions may change; the vision does not.[1]

Balcony vs. the Dance Floor: When you're "on the dance floor," you are in the middle of the chaos. You can only see what is around you at a given moment. Getting to the "balcony" gives you perspective; it allows you to see the bigger picture.[2] Think of the old chestnut, "You can't see the forest for the trees;" the dance floor is the trees, and the balcony helps you see the forest.

Strengths-based perspective: A lens that emphasizes the good in an effort to cultivate more of it.

Before you begin:

What draws you to this element today?

What situations are happening in your professional practice that need support from this element of the framework? What guidance are you hoping for today?

Record your thoughts in the space below. Notice how they change over time as you return to this element.

Date	Notes

Coaching Session 3

Coach: What's the most important thing for us to talk about today?

School Leader: I'm a little frustrated right now.

Coach: Go on….

School Leader: I just don't understand why my teachers can't see the big picture! I keep trying to show them the connections, but all they say is, "Now you expect us to do one more thing." The irony is that I'm trying to make things EASIER for them. It's all connected!

Coach: Walk me through how we got to this point.

School Leader: I don't even know.

Coach: Think back. What triggered your current level of frustration?

School Leader: During the last strategic planning session with the senior admin team, we were looking at the most recent assessment data, and it was not what we were hoping for. So, we decided to double down on our efforts of looking at exit tickets or other formative data so maybe there wouldn't be any more surprises when it came to the state tests. We need to start building our data literacy and use this information to change instructional practices. We talked this through with our team of instructional coaches—they were on board—and then we rolled it out during the our Professional Development day last week. It did not go well…

Coach: What, specifically, did not go well?

School Leader: Well, some people are pushing back that since we didn't announce we would be using the weekly team meetings to look at data, that we have to follow the plan that was originally published. And I do understand that concern, but the data will help us better achieve the district goals that we have established. These data sessions aren't something extra; they are a way to do our jobs more effectively. I mean, schools are living and breathing institutions, and we have to be responsive to what the students need. If not, I feel like that's a disservice and is only going to widen the gaps we see! I know people are working hard, and I know they are exhausted, and I also know we have to do something to address these numbers. I'm just not sure where the breakdown is that is triggering this reaction.

Coach: So you're really upset that this new process was not well received.

School Leader: Totally.

Coach: Ok, you know what I'm going to say: my favorite Heath Brothers refrain, "What looks like resistance is often lack of clarity."[3] Let's review what you just said: you mentioned district-level administrators, data, and team meetings. Let me ask you, how much were your teachers involved in this?

School Leader: Well, our team of instructional coaches has been working regularly with our teacher teams during the after-school meeting times…

Coach: Just to clarify, were the coaches tasked with consulting the teachers to get their feedback or insights on what they need to effectively look at the data and make changes?

School Leader: Well, no,…but we did talk about how important it would be to improve our proficiency levels at the beginning of the year.

Coach: Ok, remember how we've talked about the theory of two schools: the one you think you're leading and the one where people are actually working?

School Leader: Uff, clarity. I know. I, just…I can really see how a true data culture has the potential to really help us make some significant changes. I really believe in this!

Coach: This is really important to you. I'm wondering how you might bring in more voices to better understand the different perspectives that are contributing to the resistance you feel?

School Leader: You're right. One of the things I wanted to do differently this year was to establish an Instructional Leadership Team that had representatives from our coaches, our classroom teachers, and building administrators. It just never got off the ground because of the uproar around these scores…I see now that I jumped right in, pushing my own agenda.

Coach: It's not too late! When is your next leadership team meeting? Can you start the conversation about this new instructional leadership team, then?

School Leader: It's tomorrow. I'll add this to the top of our next agenda.

Coach: How are you feeling now?

School Leader: Well, I obviously haven't talked to the coaches yet, but I feel really good about this direction. This is a collective effort, and I need to bring in more perspectives. Thank you for helping me remember that.

Analysis

"What looks like resistance is often lack of clarity." This gem from Chip and Dan Heath[3] is such a fundamentally important lesson to remember. A couple of slides during the back-to-school PD days are not enough to sustain your vision for the year. Without consistent and clear communication about the 'why' of the current initiatives or the strategic plan, things aren't going to move forward.

The "tale of two schools" the coach refers to is another classic pitfall. Believe it or not, despite numerous protocols involving sticky notes and chart paper, the results of a strategic planning session aren't always readily understood by those who weren't part of that process. In this scenario, our leader definitely seems to have clarity on the direction of their school, as well as why it's important. And, as she stated, she believes in it. This is the real work of a leader: when you can communicate your passion for the work in a way that both demystifies and inspires, THAT's when the magic will happen. Checking in on how you are making meaning for others while motivated by your vision is a crucial piece of taking a more H.U.M.A.N. approach in educational leadership.

"The education system we currently have does not do justice to our evolutionary better selves."

~Michael Fullan

Reflections in the Research

Ample literature has been written around the idea that leaders driven by an internal purpose can inspire others to make meaningful change. This is yet another way to commit to bettering our shared humanity. Leadership coaches Bob and Megan Tschannen-Moran describe a set of leaders who are driven by "things that are true, noble, reputable, authentic, compelling, gracious, beautiful, and praiseworthy."[4] For "unshakeable optimist" Simon Sinek, this is your "just cause,"[5] and for Harvard Professor J. R. Hackman it is a "compelling direction"[6] that helps people envision a new and positive future. Education researcher John Hattie states that highly successful school leaders "have developed a shared narrative about the mission [of their] school toward maximizing impact on all students."[7] This shared narrative is a powerful way for leaders to make meaning for others, making it part of a more H.U.M.A.N. approach to one's leadership style.

Think about the current initiatives you have going on in your school or district. Are these the same areas of focus from last year? Or are they brand new ideas that leave teachers asking, "Are we still doing that other thing?" As you look at your professional development calendar, is there a common throughline? Do faculty meetings and early release days build on each other? This is the root of why making meaning for others while motivated by a vision is so essential to the H.U.M.A.N. approach. As a leader, when you can help your team see the connections among what might seem like totally unrelated initiatives, you invite your team members to take ownership of their work at a higher level.

If you can do this, you can become what Liz Wiseman calls a "multiplier." Multipliers "establish a unique and highly motivating work environment where everyone has permission to think and the space to do their best work."[8] All of these ideas contribute to a sense of agency that enhances what *Human Work* authors Leanne Holdsworth and Naryan Wong refer to as "collaborative power."[9] When leaders work to build everyone's capacity, the collective humanity of our school teams increases. This will allow those in your school or district to feel like they are truly a part of something, and it will encourage your entire community to grow together.

Reflection Questions / Journal Prompts

What connections are you making to the coaching session?

Can you identify your personal purpose?

Can you identify how your purpose intertwines with the work of your school or district?

Where do you see resistance on your team, and how might you address that resistance by providing clarity?

Do you see any indications of the "tale of two schools" (the one you think you are leading and the one others actually work in) in your life?

Considering all of this, who do you want to be, next?

5 Protocols And Practices For Developing Yourself

1) Ikigai

In order to *make meaning for others while motivated by your vision*, you need to know what that vision is. Our vision is often grounded in our passions. What does your social media bio say about who you are? If you don't have a social media presence (good for you!), or you don't like what you have written and you want to change it but you're not sure how, take a moment to consider your "Ikigai."

"Ikigai" is a Japanese term for "reason for being." Authors Héctor García and Francesc Miralles[10] have written a book about this topic called *Ikigai: The Japanese Secret to a Long and Happy Life.* Ikigai seeks to find the overlap among these four areas:

- What you love
- What you are good at
- What the world needs and
- What you can be paid for

On the website, https://ikigaitest.com, you can take a free test that will help you discover what your passion is.

Spend some time reflecting here, and you might uncover the secrets to your own personal happiness, increasing your effectiveness and stability as you take a more H.U.M.A.N. approach to your leadership.

"To improve life, one must improve the quality of experience."

~Mihaly Csikszentmihalyi

2) Dance Floors and Balconies: Individual Practice

In their book *The Practice of Adaptive Leadership*, scholars Ronald Heifetz, Marty Linksy, and Alexander Grashow[2] explain the difference between "adaptive" and "technical" challenges. Technical challenges aren't necessarily easy to solve, but there is a solution; a "fix" that can be applied to help remedy the situation. Adaptive challenges, on the other hand, are those that are multi-layered, complex situations that often require a mindset shift and a new perspective in order to address them.

Remember the COVID-19 pandemic? How did your team/school/district adapt to virtual learning? How many iterations of your plan were there? How many conversations with how many people were necessary to make sure kids kept learning? And how many times were you a part of a discussion that talked about hope for the future BECAUSE of the changes you were implementing? The pandemic offered us an opportunity to make real and lasting change. Whether or not your school or district has rebounded to the status-quo that was pre-pandemic, or you have kept in place some of your new protocols because they are good for kids, the point is, that experience required you to change the way you think about education and what it "should be."

As you face your own challenges—adaptive or technical (and hopefully not another pandemic!)—Heifetz et al. recommend the process of moving from "the dance floor," where you are IN IT and can't see beyond what is happening in the next hour, to "the balcony" where you have a much broader view of the entire situation. When you are "on the balcony," you can get more information to help you understand the issue you are facing, and you might see some solutions that you couldn't when everyone was dancing around you at a frenetic pace.

"'When you part from your friend, you grieve not. For that which you love most in him may be clearer in his absence, as the mountain to the climber is clearer from the plain."

~Kahlil Gibran

Your challenge: Do you need to head up to the metaphoric balcony to make meaning of a particular situation? How does a different perspective help you reconnect with your personal vision and the bigger "why" of the work you are doing?

Also suggested for Teams

3) *Gratitude Practices*

One indicator of this element of the H.U.M.A.N. approach states: *I bring an appreciative mindset to my work. I look for the good and find moments of joy.* One way to do this is to establish a gratitude practice.

There are countless ways to do this - a quick Google search will help you uncover a variety of practices to try out, but what is most important about a gratitude practice is that the science is real. A gratitude practice can change your brain, and the impacts of this are long-lasting. Here are a few of my favorite ways to practice gratitude:

Something, Someone, Myself: I read about this idea years ago. If you are a journal writer, try noting your daily gratitude in these three categories: some THING you are grateful for; some ONE you are grateful for, and—the hardest one—something about YOURSELF you are grateful for. If you need to start out simply, that's ok. But work on taking it to a deeper level as you get more comfortable with the practice.

Framing the day: Each morning, just after the alarm goes off but before I put my feet on the floor, I say to myself, "Today is going to be a great day because I GET to….(fill in the blank)." Now, instead of waking up with anxiety and dread, I am taking control to reframe my experience.

ABCs of gratitude: I love this one to help me fall asleep. Go through the alphabet, letter by letter, and name at least one thing you are grateful for. It's a win-win: either you fall asleep before you get to "Z" or you have a wonderful list of 26 different items to take into your dreams!

Gratitude jars: Each day, write down one thing you are grateful for on a colorful slip of paper and place it in a big glass jar or vase that you can see. On the days you need some inspiration, take out a slip of paper to remind you of something wonderful. It's a gift that keeps on giving.

*Tell someone you are grateful for them — and **why***: It seems obvious, but letting someone know—unsolicited—that you are thankful for them as a human being is beneficial not just for that person, but also for you. Challenge yourself to find someone different each day to share a little magic.

> "'There's always a sunrise and always a sunset and its up to you to choose to be there for it,' said my mother. 'Put yourself in the way of beauty.'"
>
> ~Cherly Strayed

4) Word(s) Of The Year

Staying true to your purpose when the madness of our daily situations takes over can be challenging, to say the least. One way to stay grounded is through one guiding word or a *6 word story* for the year.

Choosing your "Word of the Year" isn't the same as setting a New Year's Resolution that everyone knows won't stick. It's about the power of intention (which was my word once!) and the manifestation that can come with our focus on the positive.

A quick search of the web will help you find numerous words that you might choose from, and the trick is to find what resonates with you. Physically post the word someplace (or multiple places!) where you will see it often to remind you of the power in that word and how it can impact your life. Here are a few I have used in the past:

- Intention
- Abundance
- Joy
- Trust
- Radiant
- Transformation
- Becoming

Or, you might try the poetic act of creating a *6 word story*. The *6 word story* is often attributed to Ernest Hemingway with the insanely powerful: *"For sale. Baby shoes, never worn."* If you had to create a 6 word story of what you want your year to be, what might it be? Here are two I have used:

- *Strong and confident, I am ready.*
- *This is my year to shine.*

"When a person really desires something, all the universe conspires to help that person to realize his dream."

~Paulo Coelho

One of the amazing perks of working in education is that you get 2 "New Year's Days." There is the traditional, January 1, that many others use as a day to enact change, and then there is the first day of school. You may also consider the start of the quarter/trimester/semester as well. Or the day after a long weekend. Or just any Monday. The point is, whichever day you choose, just be sure to start!

5) *Build Your Cathedral: Individual Practice*

Consider this:

> *Three men were laying bricks. The first was asked, "What are you doing?" He answered, "Laying some brick." The second man was asked, "What are you working for?" He answered, "Five dollars a day." The third man was asked, "What are you doing?" He answered, "I am helping to build a great cathedral."*
>
> *Which [person] are you?*
>
> *~Charles Schwab*

As you think about grounding in your purpose while taking on a more H.U.M.A.N. approach to your leadership, ask yourself the same questions: What are you doing? What are you working for? Feel free to jot down your ideas on the lines below.

....

....

....

....

....

....

....

....

....

....

....

"Tell me, what is it you plan to do with your one wild and precious life?"

~Mary Oliver

5 Protocols and Practices for Developing Your Team

1) Dance Floors and Balconies: Teams Edition

For a review of this concept, please visit the "Dance Floors and Balconies" for individuals in the previous section.

As you face your own challenges—adaptive or technical—Hefeitz et al.[2] recommend the process of moving from "the dance floor," where you are IN IT and can't see beyond what is happening in the next hour, to "the balcony" where you have a much broader view of the entire situation. "On the balcony," you can get more information to help you understand the issue you are facing, and you might see some solutions that you couldn't when everyone was dancing around you a a frenetic pace.

Your challenge: As a team, determine why you might need to head up to your metaphoric balcony to make meaning of a particular situation. How will a different perspective help you reconnect with the vision of your school and the bigger "why" of the work you are doing?

Here is one process you can use with your team. Together, ask these questions:

Zoom out: What are we seeing? What are all of the scenarios happening right now?
- Where is there overlap or intersection?
- Where is there redundancy?
- Is everyone aware of each person's role throughout the given situations?
- Are the right people involved in this? Who is missing?
- What emotions are coming up for people? Anger? Frustration? Why?

Action plan: What steps do we need to take to get back on track?
- Who is responsible for what?
- What is our timeline?
- What are our criteria for success?

"We can't solve problems by using the same kind of thinking we used when we created them."

~Albert Einstein

Monitor and maintain: How will we keep this going? How often should we come back to the 'balcony' to check in?

2) Leadership Stories

Storytelling is one of the most profound ways we can connect as human beings. As you think about your personal vision, look back on your life. What are 5 key moments that shaped you into the leader you are today? How have these moments contributed to the purpose that guides you in your work?

When done with teams, this activity is very helpful as you try to understand each other as individuals. It also adds context to some of our behaviors and deepens our understanding of what motivates each of us to do the work we do.

As you choose your 5 moments, consider the following:

- Were these positive or negative moments?
- What did I learn from this moment?
- Where did this moment lead me?
- How am I different because of this moment?
- If I had to go through this experience again, would I do anything different?
- How does the impact of this moment show up for me, today?

Bonus challenge: Add an artistic component to this. How might you visually represent your leadership journey? Is it a river, with waterfalls and rapids? A winding trail through the mountains or forest? A series of epic, otherworldly battles?

"Turn your wounds into wisdom."

~Oprah Winfrey

3) 5 Essential Questions For School Improvement

To stay focused on achieving your goals, it is important to regularly monitor your progress. In her book, *Data Analysis for Continuous School Improvement*, Victoria Bernhardt[11] poses these 5 questions for school teams:

1. Where are we now?
2. Where do we want to be?
3. How did we get to where we are now?
4. How are we going to get to where we want to be?
5. Is what we are doing making a difference?

As you consider the work of your teams, reflect on these questions. Bernhardt says most teams make the mistake of focusing their efforts on questions 3 and 4 (How did we get to where we are now? And how are we going to get to where we want to be?) which are definitely important ideas to consider. However, she recommends taking an "honest look" at what goes into question 1: Where are we now? by addressing these sub-questions:

- Who are we?
- How do we do business?
- How are our students doing?
- How effective are our processes?

What you find out might surprise you and take your strategic planning in a whole new direction.

"The cave we fear to enter holds the treasures that we seek."

~Joseph Campbell

4) Build Your Cathedral: Teams Edition

On your team, do you know why each of you does this work?

It's ok if you are "in it" for different reasons; the diversity of our motivations can be inspiring and mind-expanding. It's when those differences create walls or other barriers that things may become problematic.

With your team, review this parable:

Three men were laying bricks. The first was asked, "What are you doing?" He answered, "Laying some brick." The second man was asked, "What are you working for?" He answered, "Five dollars a day." The third man was asked, "What are you doing?" He answered, "I am helping to build a great cathedral."

Which [person] are you?

~Charles Schwab

- Ask each team member to reflect on the following questions: What are you doing? What are you working for?
- Ask each team member to write their answer on a sticky note, which will then be put on the wall/board/flipchart.
- As a group, review the responses. What similarities and differences do you notice? What questions arise from the team? What insights are revealed about the meaning-making processes of each team member?
- Based on what you see, where do you need to go, next?

"The stars we are given. The constellations we make."

~Rebecca Solnit

5) *After Action Review (AAR)*

The After Action Review was developed in the 1970s by the United States Army to debrief situations and learn from every crisis. It is a practice that has been adopted by safety and protection agencies worldwide, and it has been finding its way into the corporate world. In her book, *Restoring Sanity: Practices to Awaken Generosity, Creativity & Kindness in Ourselves and Our Organizations*, Margaret Wheatley[12] recommends we bring it into our schools. The goal is to come to a consensus about what happened during a particular event via the tapestry of others' interpretations. We each experience a situation through our own perspectives, and as we try to make meaning for others via a H.U.M.A.N. approach, it is essential that we are open to viewpoints that are different from our own. These discussions can lead to real changes in our behaviors, especially in our work with our teams.

Wheately[12] notes that the After Action Review, or AAR, is guided by these principles:

- It must be performed as close to the event as possible.

- Everyone who was a part of the event participates in the AAR.

- There is no hierarchy; it is accepted that each person had their own experience due to their location or level of participation in the event.

- The process is followed diligently, and all participants are allowed to speak without being interrupted or questioned.

- The lessons learned are recorded and applied immediately

A strong facilitator is needed for this process. While it is possible to find several variations on this process, according to guidance from USAID,[13] generally, the review focuses on these 4 questions:

1. What was supposed to happen?

   - Did everyone have the same understanding of the goal? Was there a clear vision for success?

   - Remind participants not to get into the details until question 2.

2. What actually happened?

   - Viewpoints will differ. This is the reason to do this. The idea is to create a very detailed picture.

   - Everyone's perspective is valid, and no one is to be questioned or challenged.

   - Allow for plenty of time for this part.

3. What went well and why?

   - This question may uncover things that were NOT planned that contributed to the success.

4. What can be improved and how?

   - This is about lessons learned. Keep a running list, and apply the new ideas immediately.

"We don't see things as they are. We see things as we are."

~Anaïs Nin

5 Resources To Keep You Learning And Growing

"What looks like resistance is often lack of clarity." This quote comes from the Heath Brothers' book, *Switch*. You can also get some insights on how to motivate people from this video parable of The Rider and The Elephant.[14] On YouTube, search for "The Elephant, The Rider and the Path - A Tale of Behavior Change" to learn more!

Simon Sinek has created a movement that helps business leaders ground in their why. He states we often are clear on the 'what' and the 'how,' but the secret is to truly understand the 'why.' You can also watch the incredibly famous TedTalk, *How Great Leaders Inspire Action*.[15]

Are you a "multiplier"or a "diminisher"? According to Liz Wiseman and The Wiseman Group, "Diminishers" are "leaders who drain intelligence, energy, and capability from the people around them," whereas "Multipliers" are "leaders who use their intelligence to amplify the smarts and capabilities of the people around them." Head to their website: https://thewisemangroup.com to take their quiz and find out!

Are you struggling to identify your purpose? Warren Berger's website https://amorebeautifulquestion.com has lots of insights and questions to help you uncover what is at your core.

How is your strategic plan coming? Do you need support breaking it down into easily understandable, actionable steps that mean something to all stakeholders? Stevenson and Weiner's *The Strategy Playbook for Educational Leaders* offers so many helpful tools and templates to bring your vision into reality.

Make Meaning For Others While Motivated By A Vision: Key Takeaways

- Know your "why" and how it connects with and enhances the why of your school or district.

- "What looks like resistance is often a lack of clarity." Help people see what you see.

- Is the school or district you think you are leading the same one that people believe they work in? Make sure you communicate your vision clearly.

Anticipate And
Acknowledge The Unknown

Anticipate And Acknowledge The Unknown

Anticipate and Acknowledge the Unknown: Leaders who take a H.U.M.A.N. approach honor the present while simultaneously and strategically anticipating the future.

- I recognize that I do not have all the answers, and I consistently embrace "the wisdom in the room."

- I acknowledge there are multiple right answers. I can move forward even in ambiguity.

- I keep my eye on the bigger picture, recognizing that decisions made today will impact the future.

- I am open to the lessons failure and setbacks bring.

- I use my store of energy and light to guide the way for others, even when the way forward is not always clear or easy.

"When I dare to be powerful to use my strength in the service of my vision, then it becomes less and less important whether I am afraid."

~Audre Lorde

Key Concepts and Definitions

Resilience: The ability to bounce back and move forward in the face of adversity or stress.[1]

Pivot: While it might be overused, being able to pivot is the ability to change course while still working toward the same goal.

Futures thinking: The process of considering all possibilities to be prepared for anything that comes.

Before you begin:

What draws you to this element today?

What situations are happening in your professional practice that need support from this element of the framework? What guidance are you hoping for today?

Record your thoughts in the space below. Notice how they change over time as you return to this element.

Date	Notes

Coaching Session 4

Coach: What's the most important thing for us to talk about today?

School Leader: I am questioning my life choices.

Coach: Say more about that.

School Leader: I just feel like everything is exploding right now. I got two more resignation letters, this presentation defending our curriculum isn't going to create itself, we have been randomly selected for a federal grant use audit, and with the upcoming school board election, I have NO IDEA who will win or how that is going to impact things. I feel like I can't move forward with anything because every time I try, I get smacked in the face with some new obstacle that wasn't there 5 minutes before. I'm exhausted, I'm not sleeping, and I feel like I am failing at leading my team through this mess.

Coach: That's a lot. You're frustrated…angry, even.

School Leader: Totally.

Coach: Let's pull back a bit and look at the bigger picture. Are you willing to do some visualization with me?

School Leader: Maybe…?

Coach: Right now, you are stuck putting out so many different fires that you have lost sight of both the progress you have made and where you are going. So, let's shift our perspective a bit, and I bet you might see that these fires are pretty localized. Ready to join me?

School Leader: Fine…

Coach: So when you look beyond the fires and the explosions and the obstacles that are smacking you in the face, what do you see?

School Leader: A scorched landscape?

Coach: Look again…and visualize what you want to see; what you know is possible.

School Leader: Ok, ok. We recruit two amazing candidates to replace the ones who are resigning. Our curriculum choices are not just accepted but well received and understood by the public. The school board election results in the most amazing, supportive new member who really believes in the work we are doing. And I am finally sleeping through the night.

Coach: Sounds like a really great place to be.

School Leader: Yeah…it does.

Coach: How has your thinking shifted? I notice that you seem a little calmer…is that accurate?

School Leader: This was a really helpful reminder that we'll all get through this. You're right, I was letting all of these fires consume me, and I took my eyes off of the goals we are working towards. We'll get through this. We always have, and we will again.

Coach: Yes, this is all part of your resilience. Our time together in these coaching sessions is also helping fuel your process of being able to show up healthy and strong. You've got this.

Analysis

Whether they are happening formally with a leadership coach or casually in the parking lot with colleagues, conversations like this one are way too common for leaders in education. When we are overwhelmed and sleep-deprived, we get stuck in "reactive" mode. This prevents us from seeing the bigger picture, blocking our ability to *anticipate and acknowledge the unknown*. As adults move through their personal journeys of development, their ability to deal with ambiguity and uncertainty expands.[2] However, situations such as the ones described in this session can also trigger states of self-protective fallback. Working with a leadership coach can provide you with a much-needed "time-out" from all of the chaos that is swirling around you. While it might seem like that's a luxury you don't have time for, I guarantee those meetings will help provide you with the insights and fortitude to be your best self for your entire community: teachers, students, and parents!

Reflections in the Research

There is a whole group of people whose job it is to predict the whims of political platforms and technological advances. Most of these individuals are not running a school full of children who have needs Right Now. But, as leaders in the world of education—where the future is literally being developed—we can't sit idly by and wait for things to happen. This requires leaders to be committed to what is unfolding in the present while also being open to whatever might come next.

The unknown can be challenging for many, as it involves what author Jennifer Abrams[3] refers to as "letting go of certainty." This is the need to seek or apply a definitive answer to both what is happening now and what might be coming next, especially in chaotic situations. This way of leading requires what Simon Sinek calls "existential flexibility," or risking the certainty of the current path "to a place that requires imagination to see."[4] However, by taking the recommendations from the authors of *Change Leadership: A Practical Guide To Transforming Our Schools*, if we trust the process to unfold,[5] the bigger picture will be revealed. Throughout all of this, Appreciative Inquiry scholars Joan McArthur-Blair and Jeanie Cockell rely on hope, for it can be a grounding force leading to new ideas during times of change.[6] This element is a call for leaders to move towards a more self-transforming way of understanding the world.

Without a sense of self and a steadfast commitment to a personal vision (see the "U" and "M" chapters for more on these ideas), sustaining the motivation necessary to lead can be physically and emotionally taxing. It calls for resilience in the face of new information or unexpected challenges. Too often, periods of transition are the norm in education. Whether it is new leadership, new teachers, or new laws and policies, the desire for some level of consistency seems to be a common refrain among leaders in education. Resilience expert Dr. Sara Truebridge[1] reminds us that resilience is about the process of bouncing back from adversity, not simply a personality trait held by a lucky few individuals. In her book, *Resilience Begins With Beliefs*, she defines resilience like this:

> [Resilience is the] dynamic and negotiated process within individuals (internal) and between individuals and their environments (external) for the resources and supports to adapt and define themselves as healthy amid adversity, threat, trauma, and/or everyday stress.

Truebridge explains the "internal process" is how we tap into our wealth of experiences to find the strength to move forward and deal with change. The external, environmental contributions are those supporters in our community that can help with this process. Teachers play a huge role in this for their students—and each other.

In their book *Habits of Resilient Educators: Strategies for Thriving During Times of Anxiety, Doubt, and Constant Change*, authors Lindsay Prendergast and Piper Lee[7] offer 9 habits of resilient educators, and each one aligns with the elements of the H.U.M.A.N. approach. Resilient educators: *clarify their why, collaborate, set high expectations, use data to drive decisions, avoid negativity, prioritize effectively, establish procedures and routines, get and use feedback, and set goals.* All of this reinforces the idea that "resilience" is an ongoing and sustained developmental process that allows us to maintain our strong and vibrant physical and mental wellness despite the chaos that is happening around us, a.k.a. the life of a school leader.

Unfortunately, when faced with uncertainty or anxiety around the unknown, leaders may attempt to make meaning of their limited data by creating stories to explain what is not explainable. Jennifer Garvey Berger[8] identifies these limiting stories as potential mindtraps that can block one's development. Brené Brown[9] suggests checking these stories for accuracy to ensure they are not limiting one's viewpoint. At times, this might require removing oneself from the frenzy of the "dance floor" and moving up and away for a "balcony view," as Ron Heifetz and his colleagues[10] recommend (see more discussion on this idea in the "M" chapter). The Arbinger Institute[11] refers to this practice as getting "out of the box" to gain distance and clarity from what presents as overly complicated and unclear. Through it all, Leadership Coaches Bob and Megan Tschannen-Moran remind leaders to engage a "spirit of wonder."[12] When put into practice, this element of the H.U.M.A.N. approach can transform the lives of leaders and, by extension, the lives within the communities they serve.

> "Look closely at the present you are constructing. It should look like the future you are dreaming."
>
> ~Alice Walker

Reflection Questions / Journal Prompts

What connections are you making to the coaching session?

Reflect back: How much change have you, your school, and/or your district experienced in the past year?

What does resilience look like for you? How do you react to change and stress? What are ways you might strengthen this process for yourself?

Considering all of this, who do you want to be, next?

5 Protocols And Practices For Developing Yourself

1) *Understanding SCARF: Individual Practice*

The SCARF model was created by Dr. David Rock and Christine Cox, Ph.D.[13] It is a handy mnemonic that helps us understand the neuroscience of how our reactions impact how we interact with others and work on teams. The tool is fascinating, easy to use, and highly applicable to any group situation.

SCARF stands for: Status, Certainty, Autonomy, Relatedness, and Fairness. According to their research, these are the five domains that influence our behavior. By being aware of these five emotional triggers, the researchers offer a tool that allows leaders to predict behavior before an event, regulate behaviors during an event, and explain behaviors after an event, hopefully leading to greater awareness in the future. To learn more, head to https://neuroleadership.com/research/tools/nli-scarf-assessment

The next time you have a negative or unpleasant reaction to some news, consider what element of your SCARF is being activated. More often than not, multiple areas can be lit up by the same situation. As you start to monitor this, is there one area that seems to react more strongly than others on a regular basis? Paraphrased from their report,[13] here are some questions to help you understand your reaction to a certain situation via each element of SCARF:

Status: Is your level of importance on the team being questioned?

Certainty: Are you missing information that makes a situation unclear?

Autonomy: How much control do you have over the situation?

Relatedness: Does this situation disconnect you from the larger group?

Fairness: Is everyone getting equal treatment in this new situation?

Using this tool as an individual, you can help better regulate your emotional responses, which will, in turn, impact your team. Situations that connect with this element of the H.U.M.A.N. approach, *anticipating and acknowledging the unknown*, have the potential to activate all areas of one's SCARF at once! This tool reminds you to slow down, to take a "balcony view" of your reaction, and to identify the root cause. This awareness can be a light in a time when you might not be able to see the way through.

"When you walk to the edge of all the light you have and take that first step into the darkness of the unknown, you must believe that one of two things will happen: There will be something solid for you to stand upon, or, you will be taught to fly."

~Patrick Overton

2) The Eisenhower Matrix: Individual Practice

Did you know that the 34th President of the United States, Dwight Eisenhower, is often described as one of the most productive people to have ever lived? His methods have been studied, and one of his most reliable practices is what is now referred to as "The Eisenhower Matrix."

This tool will help you prioritize your tasks from NOW to NOPE. Of course, as the building or district leader, there are certainly some things that only you can do. But there are plenty of other tasks that you can probably delegate, and in the process, you can empower someone else to step into their leadership greatness. This matrix asks you to prioritize the tasks ahead of you into four categories:

Urgent and important (Tasks you will do immediately).

Examples: Aside from anything that is bleeding or involves other types of harm, visiting classrooms or writing the weekly newsletter might fall into this category

Important, but not urgent (Tasks you will schedule to do later).

Examples: Updating your faculty handbook, planning Teacher Appreciation Week events

Urgent, but not important (Tasks you will delegate to someone else since they don't require your skillset).

Examples: Many 'paperwork' tasks fall here: inputting data, monitoring the status of those annual 'required trainings' (Remember - both are important, but others can help with this. See practice #5 in this chapter's Practices and Protocols Developing Your Team for another suggestion!)

Neither urgent nor important (Tasks you will eliminate).

Examples: Responding to random sales calls for new curriculum or programs that are not aligned with your current goals. Also, take a look at your calendar; are there some meetings that you could stop attending?

When considering how as a school leader you are *anticipating and acknowledging the unknown,* this is a great tool to help you focus, by identifying where you truly need to

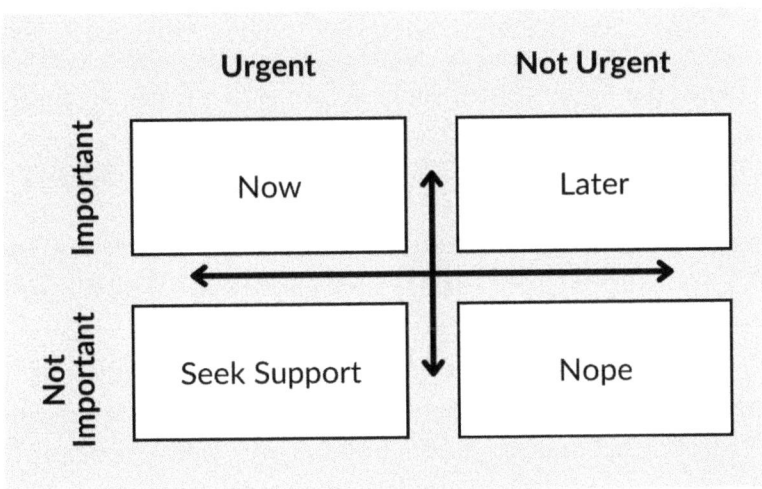

spend your time. This will help tap into your strength to lead even when the way forward isn't always clear.

So, create your template - whether it's digital or on a whiteboard where you can see it each time you walk into your office, and take a look at that To-Do list. Hopefully, this will provide you with a little more time and space to be ready for whatever unexpectedly comes your way via the next meeting or email!

**Remember, though - if you don't create the time and space to do some of the "Important, but not Urgent" tasks, they will eventually become "Important AND Urgent," which can increase anxiety.

3) *Effort And Impact Matrix: Individual Practice*

Now that you have prioritized your to-do list based on the level of urgency of each task, let's take a look at the amount of energy you are putting in to achieve the results you want. As you work to *anticipate and acknowledge the unknown,* it is essential that you maintain your store of energy and light. Noting where and how you are spending your energy will help with that.

With a reminder to always be focused on student outcomes, Sharron Helmke from *Learning Forward*[14] created a free "tool to help when everything feels urgent." You can read Helmke's accompanying article with a link to the tool at: https://learningforward.org/2023/03/23/effort-to-impact-matrix-tool

Similar to the Eisenhower Matrix, this tool also uses 4 quadrants. "Effort" runs along the horizontal axis, and "Impact" runs up the vertical axis. The quadrants are labeled this way:

> **Lower left,** *Low effort / Low impact*: While these activities might seem easy to cross off the to-do list, their impact is negligible. And instead of moving on to more meaningful tasks, we get sucked into this quadrant of feeling productive, but not actually accomplishing anything. As a leader, which of these tasks might you delegate?
>
> > *Examples might be: Spending hours on formatting: while a positive school environment is essential (see the "If These Walls Could Talk" protocol in the "H" chapter), is there someone else who can help you with signage and other visuals? Do you have a social media person who can support you?*
>
> **Upper left,** *Low effort / High impact*: These are the "quick wins." What processes are working like clockwork and are ready to be enhanced?
>
> > *Examples might be: sending a quick 'thank you' email to an individual teacher or the whole staff; bringing treats to the team meeting*
>
> **Lower right,** *High effort / Low impact*: These tasks are not worth the time. Granted, in schools, there are many paperwork/accountability processes that simply need to be completed. As a leader, though, who can help you with these?
>
> > *Examples might be: verifying attendance lists for PD hours; requiring written*

reports from teachers after attending said PD (that you now have to read and respond to!)

Upper right, *High effort / High impact*: These are major initiatives in your leadership life that will take time to see results but you know are worth it.

Examples might be: covering classes for teachers so they can do peer observations; staying ahead of new initiatives so you can model them for your teachers

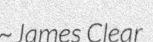

"Where you spend your attention is where you spend your life."

~James Clear

4) Mantras And Meditations

How are you feeling, physically? Are you sleeping ok? Any random, inexplicable pains or lingering colds? Oftentimes, stress and anxiety manifest in physical ways. So much of this can be traced back to the fear and the apprehension of the unknown. (*Though, of course, if something is a medical emergency, please consult a doctor!*) This is why *anticipating and acknowledging the unknown* is part of the H.U.M.A.N. approach. As leaders, when we succumb to the very human experiences of stress and anxiety, we lose our ability to process rationally or interact with others in positive and affirming ways.

There are countless apps, programs, courses, daily affirmations, and meditation practices you can try, but they only work if you can find time and space to actually do them. In his book, *10% Happier*, Dan Harris notes, "Mindfulness represents an alternative to living reactively."[15] Let's face it, too many leaders in education live in a constant state of reaction, just on this side of full-blown anxiety. Here are a few of my favorite mantras I have collected over the years that I repeat when the anxiety starts to creep a little too close:

- Trust in the Universe. Trust in Yourself.
- I am confident. I am capable.
- I am safe. I am loved.

Or, I take 5 deep breaths, squeezing my hands into a fist on the inhale, and slowly opening the fist on the exhale.

As I mentioned, there are several apps you can use with guided meditations, and I have found that a sleep meditation is a game changer. I use the free version of *The Insight Timer*. I will admit that some nights are "3 meditation" nights, but those are becoming far less frequent, and they are usually a reminder that my other anxiety reducing practices need some more attention.

"Between stimulus and response there is a space. In that space is our power to choose our response. In our response lies our growth and our freedom."

~Viktor E. Frankl

5) Tell Me More

One of the easiest ways to get caught in the anxious cycle of worry about the future is to firmly be rooted in one answer that you steadfastly believe is THE RIGHT one. When working with our colleagues, we can fall into the trap of believing our way is the only way, and that can lead to frustration and even more angst.

This aspect of the H.U.M.A.N. approach reminds us to acknowledge there are multiple right answers, and that we can move forward, even in ambiguity. Simultaneously we need to be *open to the lessons failure and setbacks bring*, as suggested in the indicators for this element. This certainly sounds like asking for a lot! But you can do both simultaneously with a little practice.

I used to work with a coach who kept a sticky note on her computer with the words, "Tell me more." This was her reminder to dig a little deeper, to get beyond the emotions clouding the initial comments to what is really at the root of the problem.

Michael Bungay Stanier, author of *The Advice Trap*[16] and other books, offers the simple advice of "staying curious longer." Far too often, our opinions are crafted before we even enter the conversation. We think we have all of the information we need, our judgments are formed, and we are ready to solve any and all problems because of our infinite wisdom (*she wrote in a sarcastic tone*). We pretend to listen, but it's only to know when it's time to insert our fully formed thoughts. By "staying curious longer," and asking Stanier's "A.W.E." question: "And what else?"[17] we can open ourselves to new insights and ideas that help build bridges between us and our colleagues. More information is a way to lessen anxiety, helping everyone move through times of uncertainty.

> "Changing how you listen means that you change how you experience relationships and the world. And if you do that, you change, well, everything."
>
> ~Otto Scharmer

5 Protocols And Practices For Developing Your Team

1) Understanding SCARF: Teams Edition

(For additional information, see "Understanding SCARF[13]: Individual Practice")

Using the SCARF model[13] with your team can help you anticipate the reactions of individual members of your team when it comes to big news or changes.

As you plan the rollout of new initiatives or how to share difficult information, review the five areas of SCARF as defined by the authors, with some questions to consider that might apply to your situation.
(Also visit https://neuroleadership.com/research/tools/nli-scarf-assessment/ to learn more)

Status: How others perceive you; your level of importance to a team or organization

> *Are positions being cut or reorganized? Will a strategic move have negative social impacts on individuals? How will others interpret the decisions being made?*

Certainty: Our need for clarity and being able to predict what will happen next

> *What information do you have that you can share? How will your team help control the spread of disinformation? How will your team acknowledge that there might be information that can't be shared, YET? How will you communicate with your team to make sure they get the information they need as it becomes available?*

Autonomy: Our perceived level of control over a situation

Is this another initiative that is happening "to" people? Who are the allies in this situation that can help others understand the rationale for decisions or changes?

Relatedness: Our perceived connection to one another

Will this new change support team dynamics or break them down? How will you set up the structures to make sure others feel a sense of connection and psychological safety during this transition?

"The language of SCARF can help us notice a threat occurring while it is happening in real time and look to regulate our emotions."

~Dr. David Rock and Christine Cox, Ph.D.

Fairness: Our perception of equal treatment within a group

We know that "fair isn't always equal." Have you reviewed the possible outcomes to make sure all groups are treated fairly? If there is a place where it is not possible, what contingencies do you have in place to deal with the fallout from people's fairness centers being activated?

2) The Eisenhower Matrix: Teams Edition

(For more information on the *Eisenhower Matrix*, see the *"Eisenhower Matrix For Individuals"* example)

Using this matrix with your team can help get clarity on what everyone is working on, as well as identify overlap and redundancy.

It is also a great way to see who needs help with what, and possibly identify new partnerships or support networks. Breaking down the siloes will also provide additional strength when unexpected roadblocks or actual emergencies arise.

When working with a team, putting the matrix on a whiteboard or other centrally located/non-virtual spot is essential. You can always convert it to digital for individual access, but the public presentation helps not just hold people accountable but generates greater support and connection. Fill in your favorite "team" cliché here (*There's no I in team; Teamwork makes the dream work*), but remember, clichés exist for a reason.

The four categories for prioritization are:

Urgent and important: What are the looming deadlines that are directly connected with your team's purpose?

Important, but not urgent: What are conversations or planning sessions your team needs to have for future endeavors?

Urgent, but not important: Think about this in relation to the purpose of your team. All the work is important, but is there another team that is better suited for a particular task?

Neither urgent nor important: Where does your team seem to spin its wheels without making any progress? Are there "assignments" where not everyone is bought in? Shelve them for the moment, and come back to them when you have more clarity.

"What is important is seldom urgent and what is urgent is seldom important."

~Dwight D. Eisenhower

3) *Effort And Impact Matrix: Teams Edition*

(For more information on this practice, see the *Effort and Impact Matrix: Individual Practice*[14])

When prioritizing tasks with your team, it is essential to look at how much energy it's going to take to achieve the desired results. Reviewing your team's list of initiatives through the "effort and impact" matrix can help you make significant changes leading to less stress and greater change. Here's how to do it:

Create your whiteboard, chart paper, or digital template with the following quadrants:

Lower left, *Low effort / Low impact*: What are the "easy" tasks you are doing that aren't really making a difference for students or teachers? (Many of these probably are done in your office...) What can you delegate?

Upper left, *Low effort / High impact*: We'd love to live here. Quick and impactful wins for teachers and students. Drop by a classroom and leave a note of thanks. Cheer on a recess basketball game. Think about things that make you love your job.

Lower right, *High effort / Low impact*: So many school initiatives fall in this quadrant. Think about mandatory lesson plans. Your teachers put in all this work, and school leaders hopefully get around to giving feedback, only to find out that those plans were not what was actually happening in the classroom, anyway. This calls for honest conversations about where we are spending our energy.

Upper right, *High effort / High impact*: These projects are definitely worth the effort IF you have the team on board to put in the work. Think about your professional development plan and the layers of support to make it happen. If you put the time and energy in, you'll see the rewards. But does your team have the time and energy? No judgment if the answer is no. Just a reminder that honest conversations with your team combined with a critical eye on your strategic plan will help you make a decision about these initiatives.

"Effort is important, but knowing where to make an effort in your life and in relationship with others makes all the difference."

~Marilyn W. Atkinson

4) On-going Formative Data Review

Does this sound like your team? You have an amazing end-of-year or beginning-of-the-year leadership retreat. You set goals, you determine progress points, and you clarify everyone's parts in the process. It feels good. You feel connected and ready to take on whatever is next.

And then the school year starts.

And all sorts of other things seem WAY more important.

That quarterly check-in meeting that was scheduled to review goals and assess progress gets bumped because of (insert pressing drama here).

Then, it starts to be "testing season," so you spend a quick faculty meeting looking at some data and making a plan to focus on the "cusp" kids; the ones who if you can just push into the proficiency band will make a huge impact for your overall school's achievement report.

And then the data comes back, and it's ok, but maybe it's not where we want it to be, so we start thinking of a new strategy to apply.

Meanwhile, those giant chart papers with all that great thinking and ambitious plans from the leadership retreat are still in the conference room…

As you *anticipate and acknowledge the unknown,* one indicator reminds us to "keep your eye on the bigger picture, recognizing that decisions made today will impact the future."

Here's a commitment I'm going to ask you to make:

> **Hold your formative data review sessions as sacred.**
> **"Inspect what you expect."**

The more anchored you can be in your plan will allow you to pivot with intentionality when things start to blow up. Let your proactiveness be greater than your reactiveness to help you *anticipate and acknowledge the unknown.* Always keep your eye on the big picture. And remember, no matter what, keep going.

> "People spend time climbing up the ladder of success only to find they are on top of the wrong building."
>
> ~Richard Rohr, Franciscan Monk

5) SOAR Analysis

Engage your team in some compassionate strategic thinking with a SOAR analysis!

Developed by Jacqueline Stavros,[18] a SOAR analysis is a tool to help conduct a look deeply at your team or organization through a lens of Appreciative Inquiry.

Appreciative Inquiry is a process developed by David Cooperrider and Suresh Srivastava,[19] and it follows the "5 D" model:

Definition: Clarify what our focus is

Discovery: Appreciate what is already working

Dream: Envision a new future

Design: Co-construct a plan to achieve this future

Destiny: Implement the design, and continue to innovate!

Many people have heard of the business-oriented SWOT analysis: (*Strengths-Weaknesses-Opportunities-Threats*). The SOAR analysis aims to shine a light on where things are going well, and how to create even more experiences for the team or organization to shine. When considering how we are flexing our compassion muscles, aiming to understand our collective experience is essential. The SOAR analysis is a way to move beyond negativity and into a positive mindframe that welcomes individual perspectives on the greater whole.

Here are some guiding questions that focus on schools (you can find even more resources on https://www.soar-strategy.com):

Strengths: What is working really well for us? Where do we shine? Think students, teachers, and community relations.

Opportunities: Where are the opportunities to see even greater success? Where are the sparks we can fan into flames?

Aspirations: Who do we want to be as a school and a district? What is the legacy we want to leave?

Results: Look into the future: What does success look like for us?

Anticipate And Acknowledge The Unknown: Key Takeaways

- "Resilience" is a process, not a trait. It's not a characteristic you either have or don't; it is the ability to bounce back and move forward in the face of adversity or stress.

- The anxiety that comes with change can be debilitating. Personal and professional mindfulness and planning can help.

- It is essential to be in the 'now' regarding what is happening in school or district, but you must also keep an eye on where you are going and what is coming.

5 Resources To Keep You Learning And Growing

If you have ever been told, "Hope is not a strategy," this book asks you to reconsider that notion. Authors Michelle L. Trujillo, Douglas Fisher, and Nancy Frey of *Teaching and Learning in the Face of Adversity* believe that as educators, we need to "ignite hope" in our students and ourselves in order to move through whatever adversity our world is facing. This book offers you practical strategies and reflection points to use with yourself and your teams!

Sara Truebridge's book, *Resilience Begins with Beliefs*, helps us understand how resilience is a process, not a trait. We all have had personal experiences that help us be strong in moments of difficulty. As educators, communicating our belief in our students' resilience can have a significantly positive impact!

Adam Grant's book, *Think Again*, as well as his podcast, Rethinking are powerful resources that help us to "embrace the joy of being wrong" and the process of unlearning and letting go of beliefs we may be holding on to a bit too tightly.

Margaret Wheatley's book, *Restoring Sanity* has several practices to engage with as you are looking to help your teams weather the storms in our political and educational landscapes. It is based on the fundamental idea that people are generous, creative, and kind - we just need to support that development.

In *Habits of Resilient Educators*, Lindsay Prendergast and Piper Lee have a collection of resilience-building strategies to help educators navigate this world of constant change. It's workbook style, with places to journal along the way!

Nurture Trust To Create
A Sense Of Belonging

Nurture Trust To Create A Sense Of Belonging

Nurture Trust to Create a Sense of Belonging: Leaders who take a H.U.M.A.N. approach empathetically nurture spaces where individuals and teams can thrive.

- I use kindness and compassion to strengthen my connections to create a culture of inclusion of belonging.

- I cultivate spaces where others feel psychologically safe and inspired to do their best.

- I embrace my role as a positive and productive team member.

- I seek to understand others I work with, even when I may not agree.

- I strive to create the conditions that build the capacities of individuals that contribute to a greater vision.

"As educators in a human-centered field, we live out loud our elemental beliefs in the worth and dignity of all human beings."

~Jennifer Abrams

Key Concepts and Definitions

Psychological Safety: Based on Amy Edmondson's[1] work, the idea that people feel comfortable sharing their opinions, asking questions, and taking risks.

Trust: From FranklinCovey[2]: *"The confidence that results from one's character and competence."*

Belonging: From Floyd Cobb & John Krownapple[3]: *"The feeling that one has when intentional acts of inclusion allow someone to feel validated, appreciated, accepted, and treated fairly."*

Inclusion: The intentional actions a team or organization takes to help people feel welcome and appreciated. Acts of inclusion result in a sense of belonging.

Building capacity: The intentional focus placed on helping teachers grow as both professionals and human beings. This can be in their instructional practices or their social-emotional development (collaborating, for example).

Before you begin:

What draws you to this element today?

What situations are happening in your professional practice that need support from this element of the framework? What guidance are you hoping for today?

Record your thoughts in the space below. Notice how they change over time as you return to this element.

Date	Notes

Coaching Session 5

Coach: What's the most important thing for us to talk about today?

School Leader: I just got our culture survey results back. They are a little grim.

Coach: Say more about that.

School Leader: Well, our student numbers are OK; the majority of kids feel like they have an adult they can go to, and most feel safe at school

Coach: And...?

School Leader: It's our staff results. Only 47% of staff agree the culture is positive, and 68% say they do not feel connected to the larger community. This is just not ok. I mean, how are we supposed to model these practices for our students if we are failing each other in the adult community?

Coach: That is really tough feedback. Why do you think they might feel that way?

School Leader: I'm not sure; this external survey didn't allow for written comments. We say we are trying to be inclusive, but I can see how the groups form. The same people talking to the same people; the same seats at the faculty meetings...I hate to say it, but sometimes, it feels like there isn't a lot of trust among the staff. This isn't the culture I want to have here.

Coach: Wow. These are really important insights and observations. What are some ideas you have that might help people bridge their differences and start making connections with one another?

School Leader: I think we need to have an honest conversation with everyone about who we want to be as a collective staff. We need to take a hard look at the behaviors we are modeling versus those we want to model for our students. I mean, the kids are ALWAYS watching, and we need to be better...not just for our students, for each other, too.

Coach: Absolutely. So where to start?

School Leader: I think I need to start with some "customer research." Maybe I can create a follow-up survey to get insights from my teachers. I HOPE people feel psychologically safe enough to share their honest feelings with me about how we can be better.

Coach: A follow-up survey sounds like a great idea. Shall we generate some questions?

School Leader: Yes! I can then hopefully explain the rationale and launch the survey at next week's faculty meeting.

Coach: Would you like support in crafting your message to the faculty? And, then, after you get the results, we can review the data together at our next session, and work on your next steps?

School Leader: Both of those things would be awesome. Thank you!

Analysis

The adult cultures of a school matter far more than we realize. We work so hard to cultivate a sense of belonging for our students, sometimes, we make the assumption that the adults will be *fine* no matter what. They are adults after all, aren't they? Shouldn't they already know how to play nicely with one another? All too often, behaviors that would never be acceptable in a classroom run rampant in the staff room. This work we do is hard; it is complicated, emotional, and messy. And yet, it can also be full of joy and laughter and possibility. As leaders, how do we cultivate more of this positivity—and not in the toxic sense, but in a way that truly allows people to feel seen and valued in a way that encourages them to thrive? Trusting those who are different from us can contribute to our growth and development of adults. To do this requires embracing a level of emotional intelligence that focuses on our shared humanity. In today's highly volatile political climate, the need to *nurture trust to create a sense of belonging* via a H.U.M.A.N. approach is stronger than ever. The support of a leadership coach can help school and district leaders sort through the noise in order to take actions that result in a culture that is inclusive and safe for everyone.

Reflections in the Research

More and more research is surfacing around the idea that leaders working towards a better humanity empathetically nurture spaces where individuals and teams can thrive. Included in this collection is John Hattie's[4] work concerning student achievement that reveals high-impact school leaders commit to building trust and relationships. As adults move through their journeys of individual development, they gain the tools needed to create an inclusive culture. Organizational experts Lee Bolman and Terrence Deal[5] recognized that "love" is a gift of leadership that is manifested when we take the time to truly know and understand others. This component of understanding leads to trust.

Trust is essential in nurturing relationships and creating strong teams. Trust is measured in how much confidence people have in you as a result of your actions and your intelligence. Leadership expert Ken Blanchard provides a handy mnemonic via the *ABCDs of Trust* to ground this work: leaders must be **a**ble, **b**elievable, **c**onnected, and **d**ependable.[6]

When there is trust, greater opportunities for collaboration emerge,[7,8] which can lead to new possibilities for individuals and teams.[9] This newfound sense of agency and empowerment yields greater collective efficacy. Collective efficacy[10] is the "enhanced confidence to overcome any barriers and limitations," which fuels our resilience processes. Linda Lambert and colleagues remind us that "leadership is evolving into an interdependence of relationships,"[11] making a leader's commitment to their own trustworthiness and developing the trust within their teams essential.

Psychologically safe spaces where people can ask questions and disagree without fear of repercussion or reprimand are a hallmark of effective teams.[1] Sometimes, this looks like abandoning the need to agree with teammates or colleagues when it only serves a peacekeeping purpose.[12,13] Brené Brown[13] notes this via the language of "power with" versus "power over." "Power with" is nurturing and supportive, whereas "power over" implies directives to be fearfully followed. Emotional Intelligence experts Daniel Goleman et al.[14] add to this conversation by noting that "power with" can look like assuming a coaching stance that communicates a belief in people and strengthens teams. When school leaders embrace the responsibility of nurturing trust to create a sense of belonging, they must also explicitly commit to serving all learners—including the adults—with a sense of dignity.[15] All of these inclusive actions and ideals comprise the final element of the H.U.M.A.N. approach.

Reflection Questions / Journal Prompts

What connections are you making to the coaching session?

How would you rate your personal sense of belonging to your school? To your district?

What does belonging look and feel like for you?

How are you working to intentionally create a culture of psychological safety?

Considering all of this, who do you want to be, next?

5 Protocols And Practices For Developing Yourself

1) Heliotropic Leadership

Have you ever seen a video of a sunflower following the sun? It is beautiful and powerful to watch, and the concept reflects a specific leadership attribute.

It wasn't until recently that I learned about "Heliotropic Leadership." The word itself, "heliotrope," comes from the Greek words "helio," for sun, and "trepin," to turn. The word is meant to describe plants turning toward the sun.

Kim Cameron, a leading theorist in this field, applied it to leadership. He describes it as a style of leadership that is committed to providing a positive environment that leads to growth. Cameron writes:

> *Physiologically speaking, evidence suggests that human beings are dependent on and are inherently inclined toward light and toward the resultant positive energy to thrive.*[16]

I love the image of leaders as a light-giving and life-sustaining force. When nurturing a sense of trust and belonging, this type of leadership is essential.

Harry Cohen,[17] another proponent of Heliotropic Leadership, reminds people to "**be the sun, not the salt**." Visit https://bethesunnotthesalt.com/video to watch a video about what that means. How might you use this practice to nurture trust and a sense of belonging in your sphere of influence?

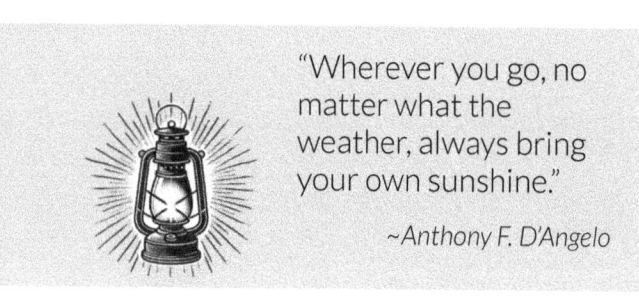

"Wherever you go, no matter what the weather, always bring your own sunshine."

~Anthony F. D'Angelo

2) Well-being Check-In: Individual Practice

Michelle Trujillo, co-founder of the Center for Learning and Well-being, offers a check-in tool to determine a baseline for social-emotional well-being for educators. During a CASEL (Center for Academic, Social, and Emotional Learning) webinar, she said this:

> We expect our teachers to be able to teach [SEL] skills. Still, if we aren't supporting the educators in living out the skills themselves and becoming aware of what they are and how they develop them, then we're not doing our job in supporting our educators, so they can't do their job in supporting their students.[18]

I couldn't agree more! When we are regulated in our emotional state, people feel safer around us. As noted previously, psychological safety engenders trust, and when people trust, they begin to feel like they belong.

Trujillo's "Baseline Social Emotional Well-being Check-In" offers a series of statements for you to consider how **reflective, intentional, empathetic, connected, accountable, and equitable** your daily experiences are. Visit https://kristenmoreland.com to get the check-in, and be sure to head to Trujillo's website https://centerforlearningandwellbeing.org to learn about her book *Social Emotional Well-being for Educators*[19] and so much more information!

As you review your responses to the statements on the "Baseline Social-Emotional Well-being Check-In," consider:

- Which category, in general, is the most natural for you?
- Which category, in general, is the most challenging for you?
- What does this information tell you about how you are nurturing a culture of trust and belonging?

Assess your personal state, first. Then head to the "Teams Edition" for a protocol to use with those you support as you work to create a culture of trust and belonging.

"I will not let anyone walk through my mind with their dirty feet."

~Mahatma Gandhi

3) How Trustworthy Are You?

Trust experts at FranklinCovey[2] define trust as the "**confidence born of one's character and competence**." Trust, like change, is a genre in its own right as far as the wealth of books and resources available that can help you become more trustworthy as a leader. Higher levels of trust lead to higher levels of productivity and positivity.

Susan Stephenson, author of *Leading with Trust: How to Build Strong School Teams*,[20] offers a wealth of resources to help leaders look at the whole picture regarding the level of trust in their schools. Stephenson reminds us of the very important act of assessing the school's history to consider how past events impact the current state. If people are constantly anxious or have the "I just need to keep my head down" mentality, chances are, there is some unresolved trauma there from past experiences. Unfortunately, those experiences were probably due to decisions made by past leaders.

Want some insights into just how trustworthy you are? Stephenson has a free self-assessment for leaders that asks you to reflect on the current state of your school. By looking through the proverbial window at the world around you, you can then turn the mirror back to yourself to see how your score aligns with the perception you have of yourself.

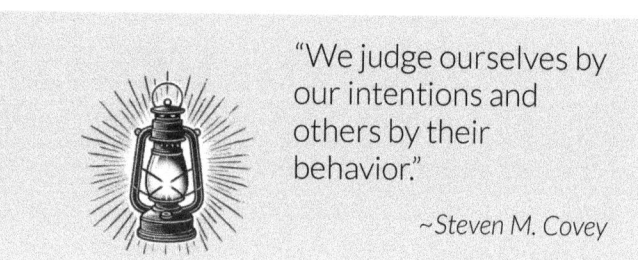

"We judge ourselves by our intentions and others by their behavior."

~Steven M. Covey

To access the self-assessment, go to: https://solutiontree.com and search their free resources!

4) Build your Emotional Intelligence (EI)

Emotional Intelligence (EI) is both an individual and a group characteristic. Daniel Goleman et al.[14] claim that a leader's mood impacts everyone else's emotions. We all know what this is like; have you ever warned a colleague that today might not be a good day to ask for something? We can see others' behaviors so clearly, yet how clearly do we see our own?

Understanding the impact of our emotional state is a way to be emotionally intelligent. The updated four domains of emotional intelligence, as discussed in Goleman et al.'s *Primal Leadership*, are **self-awareness, self-management, social awareness, and relationship management**.

Many of the practices and protocols suggested in this book help build your emotional intelligence. From recognizing your triggers and understanding what "fallback" looks like for you, to actively listening to others in order to really connect. Your emotional intelligence as a leader is foundational to the acts of nurturing trust and a sense of belonging. Those with low levels of EI will struggle in this area, but if you have been engaging in these suggested practices and protocols, you are well on your way to genius-level emotional intelligence!

Here's one more practice for you to try:

Journaling.

You can go all out in the "Dear Diary" sense, or, you can take it down to just a few moments of reflection in each of the EI domains. If you can do this consistently, you may start to notice patterns, which will increase your level of EI. Here are some basic prompts you can use at the close of each day:

- What is something I am proud of from today?
- How did I manage my emotions today?
- What did I learn about my team today?
- What was a success I had with my team today?

Choose 1 or reflect on all 4! There is no wrong way to do this. But, just like our compassion muscles, our emotional intelligence needs exercise every day in order to strengthen and thrive. You've got this!

> "Emotional maturity doesn't come with age. It comes from self awareness."
>
> ~ Tory Eletto

5) When Trust Is Broken

In the opening coaching session for this section, our school leader was realizing that there didn't seem to be a lot of trust among the faculty. Paying attention to our interactions with each other takes a clear commitment, and it is not a "one-and-done" kind of situation. This is why this element of the H.U.M.A.N. approach uses the verb "nurture."

Throughout these pages, there have been many suggestions for activities that can strengthen our relationships with one another. This is the foundation of trust. But what happens when there is a significant event that breaks the trust that has been established? Or, what if trust has been slowly eroding over time, via a series of small moments that have been compounding on each other? How do you lead your team or faculty back to a place where they can trust their leader and each other?

As the leader, reflect on these questions:

Do you need a culture "re-set"?

Is there something that you need to apologize for? Have there been some unintended consequences of a decision that requires a transparent explanation?

If yes, find the time to publicly address the situation. If one person has lost trust, it's highly likely others have, too.

Whose voice has been missing lately?

When your allies go quiet, that is an indication that something is out of alignment. Who do you need to connect with? That person or people might be waiting for you to come to them to ask for their insights. Just remember to be all-in with your listening. (For more on listening, refer to the "H" chapter.)

"Almost everything will work again if you unplug it for a few minutes...including you."

~Anne Lamott

Keeping your finger on the pulse of your school or district culture is a massive key to success. It's a human business we're in, and humans can be messy. But with honesty, compassion, and a commitment to a positive culture, trust CAN be rebuilt, even if it has been broken. Be patient, and know you are on the right path!

5 Protocols And Practices For Developing Your Team

1) Well-being Check-In: Teams Edition

(For more background on Michelle Trujillo's work, please see the "Well-being Check-In: Individual Practice")

Michelle Trujillo's "Baseline Social-Emotional Well-being Check-In"[19] offers a series of statements for you to consider how reflective, intentional, empathetic, connected, accountable, and equitable your daily experiences are. Visit https://kristenmoreland.com for the free self-assessment, and get the book, Social Emotional Well-being for Educators, for so much more information!

If you are using this with your teams, try this protocol:

Engage your team in a **Small Fire discussion group**. (*See "U" | Protocols And Practices For Developing Your Team | #2 for the step-by-step directions on how to set this up.*)

Round 1: Share a statement that you rated as "Very Natural For Me," and explain why.

Round 2: Share a statement you rated as either "Challenging" or "Very Challenging" and explain why.

Round 3: Share your thoughts on how you want to bring these ideas back to your immediate sphere of influence (principals or assistant principals back in their school; teacher leaders back to their grade level or content teams, etc.)

One facilitation note: These can be very vulnerable conversations. And to be vulnerable, people need to feel a sense of psychological safety. All of this is rooted in trust. Set clear norms around confidentiality, and invite people to share only as much as they are comfortable. These are two small ways to demonstrate your own trustworthiness as a leader.

"The secret is to not allow the fact that you can't do everything keep you from doing something. Something, then rest. Something, then rest."

~Glennon Doyle

2) Self-Portraits

Taking the time to learn about who the members of our team are is a great way to build trust and nurture a sense of belonging. To this end, I love a good self-portrait exercise! With a strong sense of psychological safety, these self-portraits can reveal so much and allow for connections you may have never considered before. You can tweak this however you want, but here's one of my go-to templates:

As the facilitator, you can create your own 'stick figure' outline, or feel free to use this one (head to https://kristenmoreland.com for the template!). Then, ask your participants to either write, draw, find images from magazines, or use craft materials (pipe cleaners, cotton balls, googly eyes, glitter pens, felt squares) to express their answers to the questions below.

People can be as literal or as metaphorical as they want, and again, higher levels of trust will contribute to deeper responses.

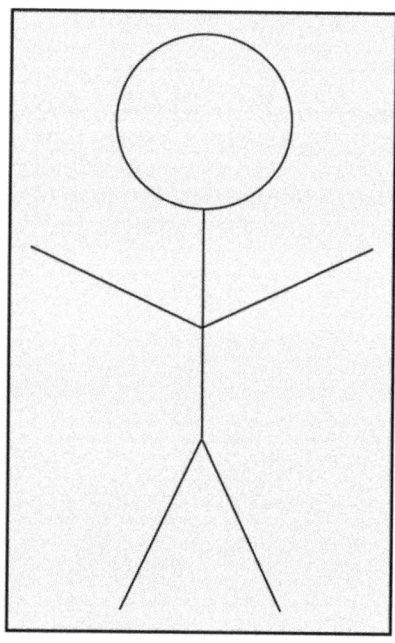

Head: What kind of thinker are you?

Heart: What are you guiding / foundational beliefs?

Left hand: What do you bring to the team?

Right hand: Where might you lead this team?

Left foot: Where do you come from?

Right foot: Where are you going?

After each participant shares their self-portrait, allow time for others to make connections to what has been shared, or offer a kind word validating the presenter. Throughout the process, take some time to observe: what connections are your team members making among each other? Are new relationships created? Existing relationships deepened? How does this level of vulnerability support the culture of trust within your team?

3) *Precious Objects*

Similar to the self-portraits activity in Practice #2, "precious objects" are another wonderful way to get to know people and encourage a sense of belonging. The story doesn't have to be long (though you may want to suggest a time limit so all participants can have equal air time) and give the person who is sharing your full attention. Be sure to allow time for participants to share connections and validations when the presenter is finished. These are the moments that enhance your connections with one another. There are countless variations on this protocol; here are a few you might try:

Share a precious object that represents:

- Your non-school life
- Who you are as an educator
- A personal growth goal you have for this year
- A professional growth goal you have for this year
- Your childhood
- Your cultural heritage
- A significant lesson you have learned in your life
- A significant achievement you have made in your life
- Your future goals and aspirations
- What you value most in your life
- Something you have carried with you for quite some time

"So this, I believe, is the central question upon which all creative living hinges: Do you have the courage to bring forth the treasures that are hidden within you?"

~Elizabeth Gilbert

4) *Moments That Change You*

In the fall of 1995, I was 21 years old and considering what to do with my life after I graduated from college. Though I would be doing my student teaching in the spring, I wasn't quite ready to jump full-time into a classroom. I wanted to see the world, but I also needed some money to make that happen. Sharing these thoughts with a friend over coffee, he revealed similar doubts about his next steps. Though I don't remember the exact words, he said something to the effect of, "I think I'll just join the Peace Corps like my friend-from-high school's parents did." And I thought, The Peace Corps! That's a fantastic idea! And I applied the next day. Right after graduation, I headed off to Cameroon to serve as a TEFL (Teaching English as a Foreign Language) volunteer for 2 years.

That cup of coffee changed my life. (And I actually married that high school friend whose parents were in the Peace Corps!)

Whether you call it fate, or kismet, or just a coincidence, there are moments when someone says something or does something that causes you to make a decision that takes your life in a totally different direction. Far too often, those people have no idea what they put in motion.

One way to engender a sense of belonging on your team is to let people know how they have positively impacted you. Now, it might not be something that led you to another country, but maybe someone recommended a book, or a podcast, or a T.V. show that has caused you to think about things differently. Or, maybe someone described a vacation adventure that caused you to take a risk and pursue something new! Whatever it was, let your colleague know. I promise it will have a positive impact!

Here's a practice to try with your team:

Step 1: Ask your team to think about something nice, or unexpected, or out of the ordinary that someone else on the team did for them that made a difference.

Step 2: Write a thank-you note to that person. Not an email, not a text, but a hand-written thank you note (*facilitation move: make sure you have some thank you notes on hand for this activity*).

Step 3: Open the floor for folks to share. You don't need to hear from everyone, but even if the team hears just one or two stories, that might be its own "sliding door moment."

Step 4: Make this an ongoing practice with your people. Reserve 5 minutes of each team meeting to share your appreciations of one another.

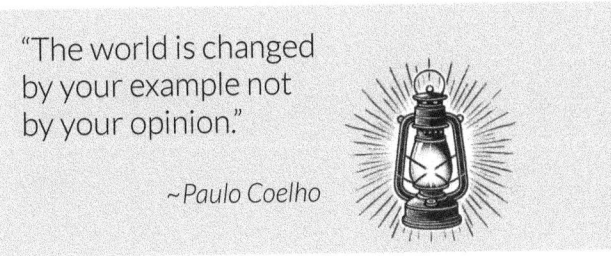

"The world is changed by your example not by your opinion."

~Paulo Coelho

5) Find Your Marigolds

Many schools or districts tend to have some kind of mentoring program, or "buddy teacher" for those who are new to the team. This person is often there to help you find the bathroom, use the photocopier, and maybe share other inside information like where to park and who keeps the best stash of chocolate. Once the new person has acclimated, they tend to find their "work friends;" maybe those on the same grade level or in the same department. *Cult of Pedagogy* creator Jennifer Gonzalez[21] offers this piece of advice for new teachers as they are looking for "their people:" find your marigold.

In her blog post, *Find your Marigold: The One Essential Rule for New Teachers*, Jennifer Gonzalez explains the "Marigold Effect" in gardening this way:

> *Many experienced gardeners follow a concept called companion planting: placing certain vegetables and plants near each other to improve growth for one or both plants. For example, rose growers plant garlic near their roses because it repels bugs and prevents fungal diseases. Among companion plants, the marigold is one of the best: It protects a wide variety of plants from pests and harmful weeds. If you plant a marigold beside most any garden vegetable, that vegetable will grow big and strong and healthy, protected and encouraged by its marigold.*

You can read the whole post at https://cultofpedagogy.com/marigolds

But this advice isn't just for new teachers to the profession: it can be applied to teachers everywhere, at any point in their career. We all know that there are plenty of human beings who function as "marigolds," helping others to flourish (and those who take a more H.U.M.A.N. approach to their leadership embody these characteristics, too!).

Here's the practice:

- Identify who the "Marigolds" are on your staff.

- Thank them for being such positive and supportive contributors to your culture.

- Invite them to be mentors or to step into other key leadership roles that will allow their impact to spread.

THEN - here's the challenge. Have an honest and reflective conversation with your team. How is each of you showing up in a way that promotes and *nurtures trust to create a sense of belonging* for everyone?

"Whatever makes you feel the sun from the inside out, chase that."

~Gemma Troy

5 Resources to Keep You Learning and Growing

Amy Edmondson's work, *The Fearless Organization: Creating Psychological Safety in the Workplace for Learning, Innovation, and Growth,* explains how to create psychological safety in your teams and organizations. "Success requires a continuous influx of new ideas, new challenges, and critical thought, and the interpersonal climate must not suppress, silence, ridicule or intimidate." When there is a culture of trust and belonging, psychological safety is present as well.

In their *Belonging Through a Culture of Dignity*, Floyd Cobb and John Krownapple spell out exactly what it means to belong, and how educators can deepen their understanding of this fundamental element of educational equity in order to make real change in their schools. It's a powerful read!

DEI Deconstructed is one of the most informative DEI books I have read in a long time. The author creates a clear picture of what "best practices" in the field are today. It offers a clear, experience and research-based path for others to follow when leading this incredibly important work.

The Culture Code and its accompanying playbook are classics in the genre of organizational development. Daniel Coyle reminds us that "Culture is not something you are. It's something you do." This book offers lessons from highly effective teams that you can implement in your own school.

"We must connect WITH people and TO purpose." In *Trust & Inspire*, Steven Covey offers leaders an alternative to the "command and control" style of leadership: trust and inspire. This style of leadership is grounded in the idea that people are "creative, collaborative, and full of potential." With these beliefs, a sense of belonging is imminent.

Nurture Trust to Create a Sense of Belonging: Key Takeaways

A *sense* of belonging is just that – it's a feeling others have because of the work we do. We have to take intentional actions to create the conditions where people feel like they belong.

One way to do this is by building trust. Different experts have different ideas on the key components, but one thing is clear: building relationships is essential.

How do you build relationships? Listen to people. Connect with them. Prove to them that you are there for them, that you see them, and that they are valued for who they are and what they bring.

Operationalizing Our Commitment

A H.U.M.A.N. approach to educational leadership is essential. While widely written about in various contexts, all of the ideas presented here represent an aspirational state for today's leaders in education. The H.U.M.A.N. approach to educational leadership is not a magic wand but a call to action to increase our shared humanity inside and outside the walls of today's schools.

While the world will continue to change, there will always be human beings in our schools. Creating intentional spaces that nurture the kind of adults who will positively impact our collective humanity needs to be the primary focus for educators. When political battles rage in a community, Margaret Wheatley shares these words for those on the front lines: "My aspiration for you is to see clearly so you may act wisely."[1] Seeing more of the nuances that exist in the fabric of our humanity as we work to learn and unlearn will help us embrace the ongoing state of "becoming." Through leadership coaching and other reflective moments, leaders in education can embrace opportunities to consider new "wise actions," hopefully resulting in greater support for the individuals we serve; kids and adults alike.

If, as a society, we truly believe in the power of education, we can use our work to elevate our collective humanity. To do this, we need leaders who **H**one their compassion, **U**nderstand their identities as leaders, can **M**ake meaning for others while motivated by a vision, **A**nticipate and acknowledge the unknown, and **N**urture trust to create a sense of belonging. When leaders in education commit to taking a more **H.U.M.A.N.** approach with their leadership, the potential for transformation is limitless.

Thank you, Dear Educator, for your commitment to our collective humanity. Thank you for being a part of this work.

> "We need to restore sanity by awakening the human spirit. We can achieve this only if we undertake the most challenging and meaningful work of our leader lives: Creating islands of sanity."
>
> ~Margaret J. Wheatley

Notes

Introduction

1. Lemov, D. (2021). *Teach like a champion. (3rd ed.).* Jossey-Bass.
2. Aguilar, E. (2024). *Arise.* Jossey-Bass.
3. Palmer, P. (2017). *The courage to teach: Exploring the inner landscape of a teacher's life, 20th Anniversary Edition.* Wiley.
4. Abrams, J. (2021). *Stretching your learning edges: Growing up at work.* MiraVia. (p. 84)
5. Ritchhart, R. (2023). *Cultures of thinking in action: 10 mindsets to transform our teaching and students' learning.* Jossey-Bass. (p. 31, p. 5)
6. Gruenert, S. & Whitaker, T. (2023). *School culture rewired: Toward a more positive and productive school for all (2nd ed.).* ASCD.
7. Goleman, D., Boyatzis, R., & McKee, A. (2013). *Primal leadership.* Harvard Business Review Press.
8. Harvard Business Publishing Corporate Learning. (2024, February). Leadership fitness: The path to developing human-centered leadership. *Perspectives.* (p. 2) https://www.harvardbusiness.org/wp-content/uploads/2024/01/Leadership-Fitness_HCL_Final-January-2024.pdf
9. Dominguez, L. (2023, February 27). Becoming a human-centered leader: Practical tips for educators. *HCLwithLianne.* https://www.linkedin.com/pulse/becoming-human-centered-leader-practical-tips-lianne-dominguez/?trackingId=P0sRlW4SRBu0YvyDZDcfUg%3D%3D
10. A few companies and individuals leading this work: *Human Centered Leadership in Healthcare* (LeClerec and Pabico, 2023); *Human Work Network* (Leanne & Naryan, 2023); *Humanistic Leadership Academy* (2023); *Human Leadership Global* (2023); *Think Human* (2023); *Gartner Firm* (2023); *WorkHuman* (2023); *Human Restoration Project* (2023); *EDLINKS* (2023); Antioch University, *The Institute for Humane Education* (2023); Wheatley, Margaret (2024). *Truly Human Leadership Podcast* (Barry-Whemiller, 2024)
11. Inspiration came from self-assessments on the websites of: BrenéBrown, Simon Sinek, Jennifer Abrams, and the Ontario Institute for Education Leadership, to name a few.
12. Brown, B. (2021). *Atlas of the heart.* Random House.
13. Strauss, C., Taylor, B.L., Gu, J., Kuyken, W, Baer, R., Jones, F., & Cavanagh, K. (2016, July). What is compassion and how can we measure it? A review of definitions and measures. *Clinical Psychology Review,* (47). 15–27. https://doi.org/10.1016/j.cpr.2016.05.004 (p. 19)

14. Covey, S., Kasperson, D., Covey, M., & Judd, G.T. (2022). *Trust and inspire*. Simon and Schuster. (p. 36)

15. Nash, J. (2023). *Be human, Lead human*. Lioncrest Publishing. (p. 17)

16. Kegan, R. & Lahey, L. (2009) *Immunity to change*. Harvard Business School Publishing Corporation. (p. 51)

17. Berger, J.G. (2013). *Changing on the job: Developing leaders for a complex world*. Stanford University Press. (p. 16)

18. Drago-Severson, E. (2009). *Leading adult learning*. Cowin / Learning Forward.

19. Thorsen, D. (Host). (2020, March 9). Robert Kegan: The five stages of adult development (and why you probably aren't stage five) [Audio Podcast Episode.]. *Emerge Podcast with Daniel Thorsen*. https://open.spotify.com/episode/7Jcu2vnGXdyAyOciUrYvT8

20. Drago-Severson, E., Blum-Stefano, J. & Lawrence, D.B. (2023). *Growing for justice*. Corwin/Learning Forward. (p. 161)

21. Parrish, S. (Host). (2020, May 26). Jennifer Garvey Berger: Creating routine in chaos. Episode #84 [Audio Podcast Episode]. *The Knowledge Project*. https://fs.blog/knowledge-project-podcast/jennifer-garvey-berger-2/

22. Livesay, V. (2022). *Leave the ghost light burning: Illuminating fallback in embrace of the fullness of you*. Kairos Publishing. (p. 11)

23. Ayers, W. (2011). *To teach: The journey of a teacher. (3rd ed.)*. Teachers College Press. (p. 37)

24. Winston School of Education and Social Policy. (2023). *Merrimack College teacher survey*. https://www.merrimack.edu/academics/education-and-social-policy/about/merrimack-college-teacher-survey/ (p.23)

25. Woulfin, S.L., Stevenson, I., & Lord, K. (2023). *Making coaching matter*. Teachers College Press. (p. 5)

26. "Given the time we have together today, what's the most important thing for us to talk about?? (p. 134). Question suggested by communication expert Susan Scott. As presented in: Knight, J. (2018). *The Impact Cycle*. Corwin.

27. Berger, J. G. (2019). *Unlocking leadership mindtraps: How to thrive in complexity*. Stanford Briefs. "Key Question: Who do I want to be next?" (p. 106).

28. National School Reform Faculty. (2022.) *What are protocols? Why use them?* https://nsrfharmony.org/whatareprotocols/

Hone Compassion

1. Lindsey, R., Robins, K.N., & Terrell, R.D. (2003). *Cultural proficiency: A Manual for school leaders (2nd ed.).* Corwin. (p.6)

2. Brown, B. (2018). *Dare to lead.* Random House Publishing Group. (p. 72)

3. Strauss, C., Taylor, B.L., Gu, J., Kuyken, W, Baer, R., Jones, F., & Cavanagh, K. (2016, July). What is compassion and how can we measure it? A review of definitions and measures. *Clinical Psychology Review, (47).* 15–27. https://doi.org/10.1016/j.cpr.2016.05.004 (p. 19)

4. Brown, B. (2021). *Atlas of the heart.* Random House. (p. 118)

5. Brooks, A.C. & Winfrey, O. (2023). *Build the life you want: The art and science of getting happier.* Portfolio / Penguin.

6. Helsing, D., Lahey, L, & Kegan, R. (2012). The implications of Robert Kegan's adult development theory for leaders [White paper]. *Adult Development and Leadership.* 1-28. Minds At Work.

7. Sinek, S. (2019). *The infinite game.* Portfolio/Penguin. (p. 174)

8. Wagner, T., Kegan, R., Lahey, L. L., Lemons, R.W., Garnier, J., Helsing, D., … Rasmussen, H. T. (2006). *Change leadership: A practical guide to transforming our schools (1st ed.).* Wiley.

9. Connors, C. D. (2020). *Emotional intelligence for the modern leader: A guide to cultivating effective leadership and organizations.* Rockbridge Press. (p. 34)

10. Bolman, L. and Deal, T. (2011). *Leading with soul.* Wiley.

11. Scharmer, C. O. (2018). *The essentials of theory u: Core principles and applications.* Berrett-Koehler Publishers, Inc. (p. 26)

12. Nash, J. (2023). *Be human, Lead human.* Lioncrest Publishing. (p. 70)

13. Holdsworth, L., Wong, N., & Friends. (2023). *Humanwork: Five leadership mindsets for humanising the workplace.* HumanWork Publishing. (p. 82)

14. Ritchhart, R. (2023). *Cultures of thinking in action: 10 mindsets to transform our teaching and students' learning.* Jossey-Bass.

15. Costa, A., Garmston, R., Ellison, J., & Hayes, C. (2012). *Cognitive coaching seminars foundation training learning guide (9th ed.).* Center for Cognitive Coaching. [Permission granted by Thinking Collaborative, LLC for limited, agreed upon use by Kristen Moreland until August, 2027]

16. How Empathetic are you? https://greatergood.berkeley.edu/quizzes/take_quiz/empathy (*This quiz originally appeared on Greater Good, the online magazine of the Greater Good Science Center at UC Berkeley) **Shared with permission.*

17. Ghost Visit. NSRF Protocols: https://www.nsrfharmony.org/

18. Fuller, R. & Shikloff, N. (2016, December 14). What great managers do daily. *Harvard Business Review.* https://hbr.org/2016/12/what-great-managers-do-daily (p. 1)
19. Roger Schwarz, *The "Sandwich Approach" Undermines Your Feedback.* (p. 1) https://hbr.org/2013/04/the-sandwich-approach-undermin
20. Adam Grant, *Stop Serving the Compliment Sandwich.* (p. 1) https://adamgrant.substack.com/p/stop-serving-the-compliment-sandwich **Shared with permission.*
21. Podcast with Adam Grant and Jennifer Garner: https://www.ted.com/podcasts/worklife/jennifer-garner-realizes-her-hidden-potential-transcript **Shared with permission.*
22. Project Zero Thinking Routines Toolbox: See Think Wonder https://pz.harvard.edu/thinking-routines#CoreThinkingRoutines
23. Simon Sinek on Empathy: https://youtu.be/c_XZ36b_aDI?feature=shared

Understand One's Identity As A Leader

1. Livesay, V. (2022). *Leave the ghost light burning: Illuminating fallback in embrace of the fullness of you.* Kairos Publishing. (p.12)
2. Fullan, M. (2021, February). The Right drivers for whole system success. *CSE Leading Education Series, 1.* Center for Strategic Education. (p. 11)
3. Scharmer, C. O. (2018). *The essentials of theory u: Core principles and applications.* Berrett-Koehler Publishers, Inc.
4. Wagner, T., Kegan, R., Lahey, L. L., Lemons, R.W., Garnier, J., Helsing, D., ... Rasmussen, H. T. (2006). *Change leadership: A practical guide to transforming our schools (1st ed.).* Wiley.
5. Kouzes, J.M., & Posner, B.Z. (2023). *The leadership challenge (7th ed.).* Jossey-Bass. (p. 5)
6. Berger, J. G. (2019). *Unlocking leadership mindtraps: How to thrive in complexity.* Stanford
7. Drago-Severson, E. (2009). *Leading adult learning.* Cowin / Learning Forward. (quote- p. 50)
8. Drago-Severson, E., Blum-Stefano, J. & Lawrence, D.B. (2023). *Growing for justice.* Corwin / Learning Forward.
9. Holdsworth, L., Wong, N., & Friends. (2023). *Humanwork: Five leadership mindsets for humanising the workplace.* HumanWork Publishing.
10. Sinek, S. (2019). *The infinite game.* Portfolio/Penguin.
11. Gomez-Leal, R., Holzer, A., Bradley, C., Berrocal-Fernandez P., & Patti, J. (2021). The relationship between emotional intelligence and leadership in school leaders: A systematic review. *Journal of Education.* https://doi.org/10.1080/0305764X.2021.197987

12. Lindsey, R., Robins, K.N., & Terrell, R.D. (2003). *Cultural proficiency: A Manual for school leaders (2nd ed.).* Corwin. (p. 6)

13. Tschannen-Moran, M., & Tschannen-Moran, B. (2017). *Evoking greatness: Coaching to bring out the best in educational leaders.* Corwin. (p. 102)

14. Brown, B. (Host). (2022, January 26). Brené and Barrett on living into our values [Audio podcast episode]. In *Unlocking Us with Brené Brown.* Parcast Network. https://brenebrown.com/podcast/living-into-our-values/

15. Denver Public Schools ASPIRE Leadership Training (2013).

16. Clear, J. (2018). *Atomic habits.* Avery. (p. 27)

17. NSRF Microlab Guidelines. (N.D.) https://www.nsrfharmony.org/

18. Grant, A. (2024, March 10). We need to talk about astrology. *Granted.* https://adamgrant.substack.com/p/we-need-to-talk-about-astrology

Make Meaning For Others While Motivated By A Vision

1. Collins, J., & Lazier, B. (2020). *BE 2.0: Turning your business into an enduring great company.* Penguin Random House.

2. Heifetz, R. A., Linsky, M., & Grashow, A. (2009). *The practice of adaptive leadership(1st ebook ed.).* Cambridge Leadership Associates.

3. Heath, C. & Heath, D. (2010). *Switch: How to change things when change Is hard.* Crown Currency. (p. 21)

4. Tschannen-Moran, M., & Tschannen-Moran, B. (2017). *Evoking greatness: Coaching to bring out the best in educational leaders.* Corwin. (p. 104)

5. Sinek, S. (2019). *The infinite game.* Portfolio/Penguin. (p. 33)

6. Hackman, J.R. (2002). *Leading teams: Setting the stage for great performance.* Harvard Business School Publishing Corporation. (p. 42)

7. Hattie, J. (2023). *Visible learning: The sequel. A synthesis of over 2100 meta-analyses relating to achievement.* Routledge. (p. 173)

8. Wiseman, L. (2017). *Multipliers, revised and updated: How the best leaders make everyone smarter.* Harper Business. (p. 36)

9. Holdsworth, L., Wong, N., & Friends. (2023). *Humanwork: Five leadership mindsets for humanising the workplace.* HumanWork Publishing. (p. 51)

10. García, H. & Miralles, F. (2017). *Ikigai: The Japanese secret to a long and happy life.* Penguin Life.

11. Bernhardt, V. (2017). *Data analysis for continuous school improvement. (4th ed.).* Routledge. (p. 13, 15) **Shared with permission

12. Wheatley, M. (2024). *Restoring sanity: Practices to awaken generosity, creativity, and kindness in ourselves and our organizations.* Berrett-Koehler Publishers.

13. USAID. (2006). *After-action reviews: Technical guidance.* https://pdf.usaid.gov/pdf_docs/PNADF360.pdf

14. The Rider and the Elephant https://youtu.be/X9KP8uiGZTs?feature=shared

15. Simon Sinek: How Great Leaders Inspire Action. https://www.ted.com/talks/simon_sinek_how_great_leaders_inspire_action?utm_campaign=tedspread&utm_medium=referral&utm_source=tedcomshare

Anticipate And Acknowledge The Unknown

1. Truebridge, S. (2014). *Resilience begins with beliefs: Building on student strengths for success in school.* Teachers College Press. (p. 12)

2. Berger, J.G. (2013). *Changing on the job: Developing leaders for a complex world.* Stanford University Press.

3. Abrams, J. (2021). *Stretching your learning edges: Growing up at work.* MiraVia.

4. Sinek, S. (2019). *The infinite game.* Portfolio/Penguin. (p. 188)

5. Wagner, T., Kegan, R., Lahey, L. L., Lemons, R.W., Garnier, J., Helsing, D., ... Rasmussen, H. T. (2006). *Change leadership: A practical guide to transforming our schools (1st ed.).* Wiley.

6. McArthur-Blair, J. & Cockell, J. (2018). *Building resilience with appreciative inquiry.* Berrett-Koehler.

7. Prendergast, L. & Lee, P. (2024). *Habits of resilient educators: Strategies for thriving during times of anxiety, doubt, and constant change.* Corwin.

8. Berger, J. G. (2019). *Unlocking leadership mindtraps: How to thrive in complexity.* Stanford Briefs.

9. Brown, B. (2018). *Dare to lead.* Random House Publishing Group.

10. Heifetz, R. A., Linsky, M., & Grashow, A. (2009). *The practice of adaptive leadership(1st ebook ed.).* Cambridge Leadership Associates.

11. Arbinger Institute. (2018). *Leadership and self-deception: Getting out of the box (3rd ed.).* Berrett-Koehler.

12. Tschannen-Moran, M., & Tschannen-Moran, B. (2017). *Evoking greatness: Coaching to bring out the best in educational leaders.* Corwin. (p. 54)

13. Rock, D. & Cox, C. (2012). SCARF® in 2012: updating the social neuroscience of collaborating with others. *NeuroLeadership Journal.* (4). Neuroleadersihp Institute (definitions from p. 2)

14. Helmke, S. (2023, March 23). A tool to help when everything feels urgent. *Learning Forward.* https://learningforward.org/2023/03/23/effort-to-impact-matrix-tool/ **Shared with permission.*

15. Harris, D. (2014). *10% happier: How I tamed the voice in my head, reduced stress without losing my edge, and found a self-help that actually works.* It Books.

16. Stanier, M.B. (2020). *The advice trap: Be humble, stay curious & change the way you lead forever.* Page Two.

17. Stanier, M.B. (2016). *The coaching habit: Say less, ask more, and change the way you lead forever.* Page Two.

18. Stavros, J. & Hinrichs, G. (2021). *Learning to SOAR: Creating strategy that inspires innovation and engagement.* SOAR Institute. **Shared with permission.*

19. Cooperrider, D. & Associates. (2012). *What is appreciative inquiry?* www.davidcooperrider.com https://www.davidcooperrider.com/ai-process

Nurture Trust To Create A Sense of Belonging

1. Edmonson, A. (2019). *The fearless organization. Creating psychological safety in the workplace for learning, innovation, and growth.* John Wiley & Sons, Inc.

2. www.franklincovey.com

3. Cobb, F. & Krownapple, J. (2019). *Belonging through a culture of dignity: The keys to successful equity implementation.* Mimi & Todd Press, Inc. (p. 99)

4. Hattie, J. (2023). *Visible learning: The sequel. A synthesis of over 2100 meta-analyses relating to achievement.* Routledge.

5. Bolman, L. and Deal, T. (2011). *Leading with soul.* Wiley.

6. Blanchard, K. (2019). *Leading at a higher level: Blanchard on leadership and creating high performing organizations. (3rd ed.).* Pearson Education, Inc. (p. 120-121)

7. Holdsworth, L., Wong, N., & Friends. (2023). *Humanwork: Five leadership mindsets for Humanising the workplace.* HumanWork Publishing.

8. Connors, C. D. (2020). *Emotional intelligence for the modern leader: A guide to cultivating effective leadership and organizations.* Rockbridge Press.

9. Wagner, T., Kegan, R., Lahey, L. L., Lemons, R.W., Garnier, J., Helsing, D., ... Rasmussen, H. T. (2006). *Change leadership: A practical guide to transforming our schools (1st ed.).* Wiley.

10. Hattie, J. & Zierer, K. (2018). *10 mindframes for visible learning: Teaching for success.* Routledge.

11. Lambert, L., Zimmerman, D. P., & Gardener, M. (2016). *Liberating leadership capacity: Pathways to educational wisdom.* Teachers College Press. (p. 9)

12. Berger, J. G. (2019). *Unlocking leadership mindtraps: How to thrive in complexity.* Stanford Briefs.

13. Brown, B. (2018). *Dare to lead.* Random House Publishing Group.

14. Goleman, D., Boyatzis, R., & McKee, A. (2013). *Primal leadership.* Harvard Business Review Press.

15. Fullan, M. (2021, February). The Right drivers for whole system success. *CSE Leading Education Series, 1.* Center for Strategic Education.

16. Cameron, K. (2021). *Positively energizing leadership: Virtuous actions and relationships that create high performance.* Berrett-Koehler Publishers. (p. 19)

17. Cohen, H. (2023). *Be the sun not the salt.* https://bethesunnotthesalt.com/

18. Collaborative for Academic, Social and Emotional Learning. (2023, June 29). *Promising practices for adult SEL.* https://casel.org/blog/promising-practices-for-adult-sel-four-part-webinar-series-part-4-recap/

19. Trujillo, M. (2022). *Social emotional well-being for educators.* Corwin. ***Shared with permission.*

20. Stephenson, S. (2009). *Leading with trust: How to build strong school teams.* Solution Tree Press. ***Shared with permission.*

21. Gonzalez, J. (2013, August 29). Find your marigolds: The one essential rule for new teachers. *Cult of Pedagogy.* https://www.cultofpedagogy.com/marigolds/ (p. 1) ***Shared with permission.*

Operationalizing Our Commitment

1. Wheatley, M. (2023). *Who do we choose to be? Facing reality, claiming leadership, restoring sanity (2nd ed.).* Berrett-Koehler Publishers. (p. 4)

References

Abrams, J. (2021). *Stretching your learning edges: Growing up at work.* MiraVia.

Aguilar, E. (2024). *Arise.* Jossey-Bass.

Aguilar, E. (2018). *The onward workbook: Daily activities to cultivate your emotional resilience and thrive.* Jossey-Bass.

Arbinger Institute. (2018). *Leadership and self-deception: Getting out of the box* (3rd ed.). Berrett-Koehler.

Ayers, W. (2011). *To teach: The journey of a teacher.* (3rd ed.). Teachers College Press.

Bass, B. & Riggio, R. (2006). *Transformational leadership.* Psychology Press.

Banerji, O. (2024, July 10). How principals are outsourcing their busywork to AI. *EducationWeek.* https://www.edweek.org/leadership/how-principals-are-outsourcing-their-busywork-to-ai/2024/07?utm_source=enl&utm_medium=eml&utm_campaign=savvypr&utm_content=bigstory&M=10651743&UUID=

Berger, J.G. (2013). *Changing on the job: Developing leaders for a complex world.* Stanford University Press.

Berger, J. G. (2019). *Unlocking leadership mindtraps: How to thrive in complexity.* Stanford Briefs.

Berger, J. G. & Coughlin, C. (2022). *Unleash your complexity genius. Growing your inner capacity to lead.* Stanford Briefs.

Berger, J. G., & Fitzgerald, C. (2002). Leadership and complexity of mind: The role of executive coaching. In C. F. Fitzgerald & J. G. Berger (Eds.), *Executive Coaching: Practices and Perspectives* (pp. 27–58). Davies-Black.

Berger, W. (2016). *A more beautiful question: The power of inquiry to spark breakthrough ideas. 10th anniversary edition.* Bloomsbury.

Bernhardt, V. (2017). *Data analysis for continuous school improvement.* (4th ed.). Routledge.

Birkeland, S., Lemons, R., Stevenson, I., & Villanova, R. (2022, April). 5 guiding questions build a strategic approach to leadership coaching. *The Learning Professional, 43*(2). 52-55.

Blanchard, K. (2019). *Leading at a higher level: Blanchard on leadership and creating high performing organizations.* (3rd ed.). Pearson Education, Inc.

Bolman, L. and Deal, T. (2011). *Leading with soul.* Wiley.

Bolman, L. G., & Deal, T. E. (2021). *Reframing organizations: Artistry, choice, and leadership* (7th ed.). John Wiley & Sons.

Brandt, R. (1992, February). On rethinking leadership: A conversation with Tom Sergiovanni. *Educational Leadership, 49*(5). pp. 46-49.

Brooks, A.C. & Winfrey, O. (2023). *Build the life you want: The art and science of getting happier.* Portfolio / Penguin.

Brown, B. (2021). *Atlas of the heart.* Random House.

Brown, B. (Host). (2022, January 26). Brené and Barrett on living into our values [Audio podcast episode]. In *Unlocking Us with Brené Brown.* Parcast Network. https://brenebrown.com/podcast/living-into-our-values/

Brown, B. (2018). *Dare to lead.* Random House Publishing Group.

Brown, B. (2023). Daring leadership assessment. *Dare to Lead Hub.* https://daretolead.brenebrown.com/assessment/

Brown, B. (2022). Living into our values. *Dare to Lead Hub.* https://brenebrown.com/resources/living-into-our-values/

Brown, J. & Wong, J. (2017, June 6). How gratitude changes you and your brain. *Greater Good Science Center.* https://greatergood.berkeley.edu/article/item/how_gratitude_changes_you_and_your_brain

Bstan-dzin-rgya-mtsho, Tutu, D., & Abrams, D. C. (2016). *The book of joy: lasting happiness in a changing world.* Avery.

Burnett, B. & Evans, D. (2016). *Designing your life.* Knopf.

Cameron, K., Dutton, J., & Quinn, R. (2003). *Positive organizational scholarship: Foundations of a new discipline.* Berrett-Koehler Publishers.

Cameron, K. (2021). *Positively energizing leadership: Virtuous actions and relationships that create high performance.* Berrett-Koehler Publishers.

Chaffe, D. (2024, May 1). Global social media statistics research summary May 2024. *Smart Insights.* https://www.smartinsights.com/social-media-marketing/social-media-strategy/new-global-social-media-research/

Clear, J. (2018). *Atomic habits.* Avery.

Cobb, F. & Krownapple, J. (2019). *Belonging through a culture of dignity: The keys to successful equity implementation.* Mimi & Todd Press, Inc.

Collaborative for Academic, Social and Emotional Learning. (2023). *SEL policy at the state level.* CASEL. https://casel.org/systemic-implementation/sel-policy-at-the-state-level/

Collaborative for Academic, Social and Emotional Learning. (2023, June 29). *Promising practices for adult SEL.* https://casel.org/blog/promising-practices-for-adult-sel-four-part-webinar-series-part-4-recap/

Collins, J., & Lazier, B. (2020). *BE 2.0: Turning your business into an enduring great company.* Penguin Random House.

Connors, C. D. (2020). *Emotional intelligence for the modern leader: A guide to cultivating effective leadership and organizations.* Rockbridge Press.

Cooperrider, D. & Associates. (2012). *What is appreciative inquiry?* www.davidcooperrider.com https://www.davidcooperrider.com/ai-process/

Cooperrider, D. & Whitney, D., & Starvos, J.N. (2008). *Appreciative inquiry handbook: For leaders of change.* (2nd ed.). Berrett-Koehler.

Costa, A., Garmston, R., Ellison, J., & Hayes, C. (2012). *Cognitive coaching seminars foundation training learning guide* (9th ed.). Center for Cognitive Coaching.

Covey, S., Kasperson, D., Covey, M., & Judd, G.T. (2022). *Trust and inspire.* Simon and Schuster.

Coyle, D. (2018). *The culture code: The secrets of highly successful groups.* Bantam.

Coyle, D. (2022). *The culture playbook: 60 highly effective actions to help your group succeed.* Bantam.

Csikszentmihalyi, M. (2008). *Flow. The psychology of optimal experience.* Harper Perennial Modern Classics.

Currey, M. (2013). *Daily rituals: How artists work.* Knopf.

Davies, B.J. & Davies, B. (2006). *Developing a model of strategic school leadership. Educational Management Administration & Leadership, 34*(1), 121-139. https://doi.org/10.1177/174114320605954

Davies, B., & Davies, B.J. (2005). *Strategic leadership reconsidered. Leadership and Policy in Schools, 4,* 241-260. https://doi.org/10.1080/15700760500244819

Deal, T. & Peterson, K. (2016). *Shaping school culture.* Jossey-Bass

DesmondTutu Peace Foundation. (2013, August 13). [DesmondTutu Peace Foundation] Ubuntu: The essence of being human [Video]. YouTube. https://youtu.be/44xbZ8MN1uk?feature=shared

Dewitt, E. (2023, February 20). Safety measure or book banning tool? K-12 obscene materials bill sparks heated debate. *New Hampshire Bulletin.* https://newhampshirebulletin.com/2023/02/20/safety-measure-or-book-banning-tool-k-12-obscene-materials-bill-sparks-heated-debate/

DeWitt, P. (2018). *Coach it further: Using the art of coaching to improve school leadership.* Corwin.

Dominguez, L. (2023, February 27). Becoming a human-centered leader: Practical tips for educators. *HCLwithLianne.* https://www.linkedin.com/pulse/becoming-human-centered-leader-practical-tips-lianne-dominguez/?trackingId=P0sRlW4SRBu0YvyDZDcfUg%3D%3D

Donohoo, J. (2017). *Collective efficacy: How educators' beliefs impact student learning.* Corwin.

Drago-Severson, E. (2009). *Leading adult learning.* Cowin / Learning Forward.

Drago-Severson, E., Blum-Stefano, J. & Lawrence, D.B. (2023). *Growing for justice.* Corwin / Learning Forward.

Edmonson, A. (2019). *The fearless organization. Creating psychological safety in the workplace for learning, innovation, and growth.* John Wiley & Sons, Inc.

EDLINKS™. (2023). EDLINKS™. https://www.edlinks.com/

Erickson, J.D. & Flewelling, J.M. (2022, August). Book review: Leadership through mentoring: The key to improving the confidence and skill of principals. *Teachers College Record.* Sage Journals. https://journals.sagepub.com/pb-assets/cmscontent/TCZ/Book%20Reviews%20Collection%202022/August%202022/Leadership-1660577002.pdf

Fullan, M. (2018). *Nuance: Why some leaders succeed and others fail.* Corwin.

Fullan, M. (2021, February). The Right drivers for whole system success. *CSE Leading Education Series, 1.* Center for Strategic Education.

Fullan, M. & Edwards, M. (2022). *Spirit work and the science of collaboration.* Corwin and AASA.

Fuller, R. & Shikloff, N. (2016, December 14). What great managers do daily. *Harvard Business Review.* https://hbr.org/2016/12/what-great-managers-do-daily

Frei, F. (2018, April). *How to build (and rebuild) trust.* [Video]. TED Conferences. https://www.ted.com/talks/frances_frei_how_to_build_and_rebuild_trust?utm_campaign=tedspread&utm_medium=referral&utm_source=tedcomshare

Frei, F & Morriss, A (2021 Winter) Trust: The foundation of leadership. *Leader to Leader (99).* 20–25.

García, H. & Miralles, F. (2017). *Ikigai: The Japanese secret to a long and happy life.* Penguin Life.

Gartner. (2023, May 31). Gartner identifies three pillars of human leadership CFOs need in an era of finance AI. *Newsroom.* https://www.gartner.com/en/newsroom/press-releases/2023-05-31-gartner-identifies-three-pillars-of-human-leadership-cfos-need-in-an-era-of-finance-ai

George, B., Sims, P., McLean, A., & Mayer, D. (2007, February). Discovering your authentic leadership. *Harvard Business Review Magazine.* https://hbr.org/2007/02/discovering-your-authentic-leadership

Gimbel, P., & Gow, P. (2023, October 5). How mentoring can help new principals lead with kindness. *District Administration.* https://districtadministration.com/how-mentoring-can-help-new-principals-lead-with-kindness/

Goleman, D., Boyatzis, R., & McKee, A. (2013). *Primal leadership.* Harvard Business Review Press.

Gomez-Leal, R., Holzer, A., Bradley, C., Berrocal-Fernandez P., & Patti, J. (2021). The relationship between emotional intelligence and leadership in school leaders: A systematic review. *Journal of Education.* https://doi.org/10.1080/0305764X.2021.197987

Gonzalez, J. (2013, August 29). Find your marigold: The one essential rule for new teachers. *Cult of Pedagogy.* https://www.cultofpedagogy.com/marigolds/

Grant, A. (2024, March 10). We need to talk about astrology: The science is clear: horoscopes are meaningless, but they aren't harmless. *Granted.* https://adamgrant.substack.com/p/we-need-to-talk-about-astrology

Grant, A. (Host). (2023, May 23). Brené Brown and Simon Sinek on the leadership skills we need to build [Audio Podcast Episode]. *ReThinking with Adam Grant.* https://www.ted.com/podcasts/rethinking-with-adam-grant/brene-brown-and-simon-sinek-on-the-leadership-skills-we-need-to-build

Grant, A. (Host) (2024, January 9). Jennifer Garner realizes her hidden potential. [Audio Podcast Epidose]. *WorkLife with Adam Grant.* https://www.ted.com/podcasts/worklife/jennifer-garner-realizes-her-hidden-potential-transcript

Grant, A. (2024, January 17). Stop serving the compliment sandwich: Criticism between two slices of bread doesn't taste as good as it looks. *Granted.* https://adamgrant.substack.com/p/stop-serving-the-compliment-sandwich

Grant, A. (2021). *Think again: The power of knowing what you don't know*. Viking.

Grant, C. & Osanloo, A. (2014). Understanding, selecting, and integrating a theoretical approach in dissertation research: Creating the blueprint for your "house." *Administrative Issues Journal: Connecting Education, Practice, and Research, 4*(2). 12-26. https://doi.org/10.5929/2014.4.2.9

Greater Good Science Center at the University of California, Berkeley. *Empathy quiz.* https://greatergood.berkeley.edu/quizzes/take_quiz/empathy

Greater Good Science Center at the University of California, Berkeley. *Greater good magazine: Science-based insights for a more meaningful life*. https://greatergood.berkeley.edu/

Gruenert, S. & Whitaker, T. (2023). *School culture rewired: Toward a more positive and productive school for all* (2nd ed.). ASCD.

Guskey, T. R. (2020). *Flip the script on change: Experience shapes teachers' attitudes and beliefs. The Learning Professional, 41*(2). 18–22. https://learningforward.org/journal/beyond-the-basics/flip-the-script-on-change/

Hackman, J.R. (2002). *Leading teams: Setting the stage for great performance*. Harvard Business School Publishing Corporation.

Harris, D. (2014). *10% happier: How I tamed the voice in my head, reduced stress without losing my edge, and found a self-help that actually works*. It Books.

Harrison, S.(2024). *New happy: Getting happiness right in a world that's got it wrong*. TarcherPerigee.

Harvard Business Publishing Corporate Learning. (2024, February). Leadership fitness: The path to developing human-centered leadership. *Perspectives*. https://www.harvardbusiness.org/wp-content/uploads/2024/01/Leadership-Fitness_HCL_Final-January-2024.pdf

Harvard Graduate School of Education. Project zero's thinking routine toolbox. *Project Zero*. https://pz.harvard.edu/thinking-routines

Hattie, J. (2023). *Visible learning: The sequel. A synthesis of over 2100 meta-analyses relating to achievement*. Routledge.

Hattie, J. & Zierer, K. (2018). *10 mindframes for visible learning: Teaching for success*. Routledge.

Heath, C. & Heath, D. (2010). *Switch: How to change things when change is hard*. Crown Currency.

Heath, C. & Heath, D. (2017). *The power of moments: Why certain experiences have extraordinary impact*. Simon and Schuster.

Heifetz, R. A., Linsky, M., & Grashow, A. (2009). *The practice of adaptive leadership* (1st ebook ed.). Cambridge Leadership Associates.

Helmke, S. (2023, March 23). A tool to help when everything feels urgent. *Learning Forward*. https://learningforward.org/2023/03/23/effort-to-impact-matrix-tool/

Helsing, D., Lahey, L., & Kegan, R. (2012). The implications of Robert Kegan's adult development theory for leaders [White paper]. *Adult Development and Leadership*. 1-28. Minds At Work.

Henley, D. (2018, October 30). 10 ways to lose your superpower at work. *Forbes.com*. https://www.forbes.com/sites/dedehenley/2018/10/17/10-self-protective-strategies-that-undo-your-super-power-at-work/?sh=4d2ba9f278eb

Holdsworth, L., Wong, N., & Friends. (2023). *Humanwork: Five leadership mindsets for humanising the workplace*. HumanWork Publishing.

Human Leadership Global (2023). *Human leadership: Inspired leaders, engaged teams, inclusive culture.* https://www.humanleadership.global/programs/

Humanistic Leadership Academy. (2023). https://humanisticleadershipacademy.org/

Human Restoration Project. (2023). https://www.humanrestorationproject.org/

Institute for Humane Education. (2023). https://humaneeducation.org/

Kegan, R. (1994). *In over our heads: The mental demands of modern life*. Harvard University Press.

Kegan, R. & Lahey, L. (2009). *Immunity to change*. Harvard Business School Publishing Corporation.

Kegan, R. & Lahey, L. (2016). *An everyone culture: Becoming a deliberately developmental organization*. Harvard Business Review Press

Killion, J. & Harrison, C. (2006). *Taking the lead: New roles for teachers and school-based coaches*. National Staff Development Council.

Knight, J. (2018). *The impact cycle*. Sage.

Kouzes, J.M., & Posner, B.Z. (2023). *The leadership challenge* (7th ed.). Jossey-Bass.

Ladson-Billings, G. (1995, Autumn). Toward a theory of culturally relevant pedagogy. *American Educational Research Journal, 32*(3(. 465-491. http://links.jstor.org/sici?sici=0002-8312%28199523%2932%3A3%3C465%3ATATOCR%3E2.0.CO%3B2-4

Lambert, L., Zimmerman, D. P., & Gardener, M. (2016). *Liberating leadership capacity: Pathways to educational wisdom.* Teachers College Press.

Landson, J. (n.d.). *I am from project.* https://iamfromproject.com/

Leanne & Naryan. (2023). *The human work network.* https://www.humanworknetwork.com/

Leclerc, L. & Pabico, C. (2023, April). Blueprints for well-being: Modeling the way through human-centered leadership and pathway to excellence. *Nursing Management.* 9-16.DOI-10.1097/01.NUMA.0000921892.27917.78

Lemov, D. (2021). *Teach like a champion.* (3rd ed.). Jossey-Bass.

Lindsey, R., Robins, K.N., & Terrell, R.D. (2003). *Cultural proficiency: A Manual for school leaders* (2nd ed.). Corwin.

Livesay, V. (2022). *Leave the ghost light burning: Illuminating fallback in embrace of the fullness of you.* Kairos Publishing.

Livesay, V. (2015). One step back, two steps forward: Fallback in human and leadership development. *Journal of Leadership Accountability and Ethics, 12(4).* 173-189. https://www.researchgate.net/publication/324452607_One_Step_Back_Two_Steps_Forward_Fallback_in_Human_and_Leadership_Development

Lyon, G. E. (n.d.) *Where I'm from.* http://www.georgeellalyon.com/where.html

Martin, R. & Osberg, S. (2015). *Getting beyond better.* Harvard Business Review Press.

McArthur-Blair, J. & Cockell, J. (2018). *Building resilience with appreciative inquiry.* Berrett-Koehler.

McCauley, C.D., Drath, W.H., Palus, C.J., O'Connor, P.M.G., & Baker, B.A. (2006, December). The use of constructive-developmental theory to advance the understanding of leadership.*The Leadership Quarterly, (17).* 634-653. https://doi.org/10.1016/j.leaqua.2006.10.006

McKean, L.E. (2024). *Compass points in a nutshell.* nsrfarmony.org. https://nsrfharmony.org/compass-points-in-a-nutshell/

Moreland, K. (2023, December 18). Adult cultures matter. *NHASCD.* https://nhascd.org/blog/

Moreland, K. (2023). *Adult cultures matter: An interpretive phenomenological analysis of a more H.U.M.A.N. approach to educational leadership* (2024. 30820467) [Doctoral Dissertation, Southern New Hampshire University]. ProQuest Dissertation & Theses.

Nash, J. (2023). *Be human, Lead human.* Lioncrest Publishing.

National School Reform Faculty. (2024). *NSRF protocols and activities... from A to Z.* https://nsrfharmony.org/protocols/

National School Reform Faculty. (2022.) *What are protocols? Why use them?* https://nsrfharmony.org/whatareprotocols/

Northouse, P.G. & Lee, M. (2021). *Leadership case studies in education* (3rd ed.). SAGE Publications, Inc.

NSRF Microlab Guidelines. (N.D.) nsrfharmony.org. https://www.nsrfharmony.org

Ontario Institute for Education Leadership. (2014). *Self assessment tool for aspiring school leaders.* www.education-leadership-ontario.ca

Palmer, P. (2017). *The courage to teach: Exploring the inner landscape of a teacher's life, 20th Anniversary Edition.* Wiley.

Parrish, S. (Host). (2018, October 16). The mental habits of effective leaders with Jennifer Garvey Berger. Episode #43 [Audio Podcast Episode]. *The Knowledge Project.* https://fs.blog/knowledge-project-podcast/jennifer-Berger/

Parrish, S. (Host). (2020, May 26). Jennifer Garvey Berger: Creating routine in chaos. Episode #84 [Audio Podcast Episode]. *The Knowledge Project.* https://fs.blog/knowledge-project-podcast-transcripts/jennifer-Berger-84/

Pink, D. (2019). *When: The scientific secrets of good timing.* Riverhead Books.

Prendergast, L. & Lee, P. (2024). *Habits of resilient educators: Strategies for thriving during times of anxiety, doubt, and constant change.* Corwin.

Procek, C. (2012). *Leading for change: How leadership styles impact teachers' experience.* (UMI 3508203) [Doctoral Dissertation, Northeastern University.] Proquest LLC. https://www.proquest.com/docview/1017707037

Project Implicit. (2011.) *Implicit Association Test.* https://implicit.harvard.edu/implicit/takeatest.html

Richardson, W., & Tavangar, H. (2023, March 29). Valuing what matters. *Big Questions Institute, Bi-Weekly Update.* bigquestions.institute.

Ritchhart, R. (2023). *Cultures of thinking in action: 10 mindsets to transform our teaching and students' learning.* Jossey-Bass.

Rock, D. & Cox, C. (2012). SCARF® in 2012: updating the social neuroscience of collaborating with others. *NeuroLeadership Journal.* (4). Neuroleadersihp Institue.

Scharmer, C. O. (2018). *The essentials of theory u: Core principles and applications.* Berrett-Koehler Publishers, Inc.

Schwartz, R. (2013, April 19). The "sandwich approach" undermines your feedback. *Harvard Business Review*. https://hbr.org/2013/04/the-sandwich-approach-undermin

Sinek, S. (2009). *How great leaders inspire action*. [Video] TedX Puget Sound. https://www.ted.com/talks/simon_sinek_how_great_leaders_inspire_action

Sinek, S. (2019). *The infinite game*. Portfolio/Penguin.

Sinek, S. [Simon Sinek]. (2018, September 21). *Leaders practice empathy*. [Video]. YouTube. https://youtu.be/c_XZ36b_aDI?feature=shared

Sinek, S. (2011). *Start with why*. Portfolio.

Slade, S. & Gallagher, A. (n.d). The case for embracing messy leadership in schools. *BTS Spark*. https://btsspark.org/blog-article/thought-leadership/the-case-for-embracing-messy-leadership-in-schools

Sonesh, S. C., Coultas, C. W., Lacerenza, C. N., Marlow, S. L., Benishek, L. E. & Salas, E. (2015). The power of coaching: a meta-analytic investigation. *Coaching: An International Journal of Theory, Research and Practice, 8*(2). 73-95. https://doi.org/10.1080/17521882.2015.1071418

Stanier, M.B. (2016). *The coaching habit: Say less, ask more, and change the way you lead forever*. Page Two.

Stavros, J. & Hinrichs, G. (2021). *Learning to SOAR: Creating strategy that inspires innovation and engagement*. SOAR Institute.

Stephenson, S. (2009). *Leading with trust: How to build strong school teams*. Solution Tree Press.

Strauss, C., Taylor, B.L., Gu, J., Kuyken, W, Baer, R., Jones, F., & Cavanagh, K. (2016, July). What is compassion and how can we measure it? A review of definitions and measures. *Clinical Psychology Review, 47*. 15–27. https://doi.org/10.1016/j.cpr.2016.05.004

Stevenson, I. & Weiner, J. (2020). *The strategy playbook for educational leaders*. Routledge.

Think Human (2022). *Think human: Unleashing the soul of your business*. https://think-human.com/leadership-development/

Thorsen, D. (Host). (2020, March 9). Robert Kegan: The five stages of adult development (and why you probably aren't stage five) [Audio Podcast Episode.]. *Emerge Podcast with Daniel Thorsen*. https://open.spotify.com/episode/7Jcu2vnGXdyAyOciUrYvT8

Tschannen-Moran, M., & Tschannen-Moran, B. (2017). *Evoking greatness: Coaching to bring out the best in educational leaders*. Corwin.

Truebridge, S. (2014). *Resilience begins with beliefs: Building on student strengths for success in school.* Teachers College Press.

Trujillo, M. (2022). *Social emotional well-being for educators.* Corwin.

Trujillo, M., Fisher, D., & Frey, N. (2024). *Teaching and learning in the face of adversity: Strategies that inspire.* Corwin.

Trusted Advisors Associates, LLC. (n.d.) *Trust quotient assessment.* https://trustsuite.trustedadvisor.com/

USAID. (2006). *After-action reviews: Technical guidance.* https://pdf.usaid.gov/pdf_docs/PNADF360.pdf

van Nieuwerburgh, C. (2012), *Coaching in education: Getting better results for students, educators and parents.* Karnac.

van Nieuwerburgh, C., Barr, M., Munro, C., Noon, H. & Arifin, D. (2020). Experiences of aspiring school principals receiving coaching as part of a leadership development programme. *International Journal of Mentoring and Coaching in Education, 9*(3). 291-306. https://www.emerald.com/insight/2046-6854.htm

Wagner, T., Kegan, R., Lahey, L. L., Lemons, R.W., Garnier, J., Helsing, D., ... Rasmussen, H. T. (2006). *Change leadership: A practical guide to transforming our schools* (1st ed.). Wiley.

Watanabe, R. (n.d.). *Leadership X adult development.* https://developingleadership.net/

Wheatley, M. (2023). *Who do we choose to be? Facing reality, claiming leadership, restoring sanity* (2nd ed.). Berrett-Koehler Publishers.

Wheatley, M. (2024). *Restoring sanity: Practices to awaken generosity, creativity, and kindness in ourselves and our organizations.* Berrett-Koehler Publishers.

Winston School of Education and Social Policy. (2023). *Merrimack College teacher survey.* https://www.merrimack.edu/academics/education-and-social-policy/about/merrimack-college-teacher-survey/

Wiseman, L. (2017). *Multipliers, revised and updated: How the best leaders make everyone smarter.* Harper Business.

Woodward, M. (2024, May 28). Artificial intelligence statistics for 2024. *Search Logistics.* https://www.searchlogistics.com/learn/statistics/artificial-intelligence-statistics/

WorkHuman. (2023). https://www.workhuman.com/

Woulfin, S.L., Stevenson, I., & Lord, K. (2023). *Making coaching matter.* Teachers College Press.

Zheng, L. (2022). *DEI Deconstructed: Your no-nonsense guide to doing the work and doing it right*. Berrett-Koehler Publishers.